Leni Fiedelmeier

6.95 BT

Dachshunds

How to Understand and Take Care of Them

Expert advice on the proper care of wirehaired, longhaired, and smooth-coated dachshunds

With color photos by well-known animal photographers

Consulting Editor: Frederic Frye, DVM

Drawings: Fritz W. Köhler·

A Barron's Pet Owner's Manual

BARRON'S

Contents

Preceding double spread: Curious and bursting with energy, these four puppies look at the world around them. They should not be separated from their mother until they are three months old.

Drawing below: Dachshunds needs plenty of exercise.

Preface

Irresistibly charming, impish, headstrong, and not easy to train: That's the abridged list of traits common to dachshunds, which continue to rank at the top of lists of the most popular dog breeds. You will find the trusting look in a dachshund's eyes is hard to resist, even when the little creature has just gotten into mischief. However, that is precisely the time when you need to be firm in disciplining the dog; otherwise, your dachshund will quickly do as it likes with you.

This updated and improved Barron's pet owner's manual, filled with illustrations, will give new owners a comprehensive introduction to all aspects of caring for a dachshund. Experienced dog owners, as well, will find new ideas and information here.

This manual will tell you exactly what to look for when buying a dachshund. It provides valuable information on care, nutrition, and diseases, along with a detailed description of the breed characteristics.

Readers interested in breeding dachshunds will find the fundamentals explained in the chapter "If Your Dog Has Puppies—Dachshund Breeding."

On special How-To pages, both words and pictures will explain what equipment and accessories a dachshund needs, what kind of care and grooming are necessary, and how you can learn to understand your pet's "language." The expert advice offered here is backed up by informative drawings and fascinating color photographs.

The editors of Barron's series of nature books wish you a great deal of pleasure with your dachshund.

Friendship between you and your dachshund does not develop automatically; it has to be earned. To achieve that goal, train your dachshund lovingly but firmly. Take its natural needs into consideration, and learn to interpret its patterns of behavior correctly.

Please read the "Important Notes" on page 63.

The Typical Dachshund— Its Disposition, Its Breed

With its irresistible charm and its roguishness, the dachshund has managed to remain at the top of the list of popular dog breeds for many years now.

Its obstinacy and "mulishness" have made it quite a celebrity among dogs— a pet that adults as well as children cherish and love.

The First Dachshund

Even during ancient times there existed a great many different kinds of dogs, the results of mutations. The image of a long-bodied, short-legged female dog with a pointed muzzle and erect ears was discovered cut in the rock of a tomb in Besheb, Egypt. It dates from the period of the Middle Kingdom in the second millennium B.C. Although there is no absolute proof that this is the direct forerunner of the dachshund, it does prove that dogs with extremely short legs and a very long back existed even then.

Why Dachshunds Have Short Legs

Originally the dachshund was bred as a hunting dog. For a long time its crooked legs were even considered especially well suited for slipping into fox and rabbit burrows and driving the animals out in front of the hunter's gun. Fortunately for the dachshund, however, people realized that these morbidly twisted legs were more of a hindrance, and a change was made in the breeding.

Why Dachshunds Are Stubborn

"Dachshunds are headstrong and never learn to obey." That is the generally accepted opinion of this little dog, and there is some measure of truth in it. A certain obstinacy is indeed one of the dachshund's character traits. Precisely this trait, however, was of great importance in the dog's function as a hunter's helper. For instance, when a dachshund was sent underground to drive a badger or a fox out of its burrow, this relentless drive to prevail was a vital necessity to the dog and the hunter. Not surprisingly, in its "pack" family, the dachshund retains this will and always insists on having its own way. All you can do is to counter this strong will with an equally strong will of your own—patiently and lovingly, but firmly.

Names, Types of Coats, Sizes

This small dog is referred to by many different names: wiener dog, frankfurter dog, German sausage dog.

They are bred with three different kinds of coats:

- smooth (shorthaired);
- wirehaired;
- longhaired.

Originally all dachshunds were shorthaired (smooth-coated); the wirehaired and longhaired varieties were developed later through selective breeding.

D achshunds quite rightly have a reputation for being self-willed and intent on achieving their objectives. It is precisely these characteristics that made their help so valuable and indispensable to hunters. When a dachshund was sent underground to drive a badger or a fox out of its den, an iron determination to prevail was essential to the dog's survival.

Father and child
This longhaired male, red (tan) with appressed silky hair, guards its puppy alertly during an outing in the yard.

Dachshunds also come in different sizes. In the United States, they are
- Standard (over 16 pounds)
- Miniature (11 pounds or less, at less than one year of age).

In Europe, size categorization varies. In Germany, for example, dachshunds have one of three sizes:
- Standard
- Miniature (dwarf) (chest up to 14 inches [35 cm] around)
- Rabbit Dachshund (chest up to 12 inches [30 cm] around).

The Ideal Dachshund

Typical features of the dachshund's outward appearance are its elongated trunk and short legs—breed characteristics that were determined 100 years ago. In subsequent decades, of course, some changes were made, finally resulting in the standard now set forth by the German Dachshund Club [DTK] and the American Kennel Club, and registered with the Federation Cynologique Internationale (FCI). Thus, uniform judging of the breed is ensured. An excerpt from that standard follows.

General Appearance

The dachshund should be low to the ground, short-legged, and long-bodied, but with compact figure and robust development; with bold and confident carriage of the head and intelligent facial expression.

Despite the shortness of the legs in comparison to the length of the trunk, a dachshund should not appear either crippled, awkward, cramped in its capacity for movement, weasel-like, or too thin.

Conformation of Body

The head is elongated and clean-cut. It should taper uniformly to the tip of the nose. The skull should be slightly arched, sloping gradually without stop (the less stop, the more typical) into the finely formed, slightly arched muzzle. The bridge bones over the eyes should be prominent. The nasal cartilage and tip of the nose are long and narrow; the nostrils are well open. The lips are tightly stretched, well covering the lower jaw but neither deep nor pointed; the corner of the mouth is not very marked. The jaws open wide and are hinged well back of the eyes. The teeth and jaw are strongly developed, with canine teeth that fit closely together.

The eyes are of medium size, oval and almond-shaped, situated at the sides, with a clear, alert, yet friendly expression; not piercing. For all coats and colors, the color of the dachshund's eyes should be lustrous dark reddish brown to blackish brown. Glassy, fishlike, or beady eyes in gray and dapple dogs are not a serious fault, but also not desirable.

The ears are set high on the head, not too far forward, long but not too long, beautifully rounded—not narrow, pointed, or folded—and flexible. The forward edge should just touch the cheek.

The neck should be fairly long, muscular, and clean-cut—not showing any dewlap on the throat. It should be held high, slightly arched in the nape, carried proudly but not stiffly.

The front, to endure the arduous exertion underground, must be correspondingly muscular, compact, deep, long, and broad. Forequarters in detail: Shoulder blade: Long, obliquely and firmly placed on the fully developed thorax, with hard but flexible muscles. Upper arm: Of the same length as the shoulder blade and at a right angle to it. Strong-boned and hard-muscled, it lies close to the ribs but is capable of moving freely. Forearm: Short, very

An address capsule that contains a slip of paper with the dog's name and the dog owner's telephone number should always be worn on the dachshund's collar.

slightly turned inward, supplied with hard and flexible muscles on the front and outside; approximately long enough for the distance between the dog and the ground to measure about one-third to one-fourth of its height at the croup (rump).

The joints between the forearm and the foot (the wrists) are somewhat closer together than the shoulder joints. The bones of the forearm, which form the wrist, when viewed from the side, should be neither stiff nor sagging. The paws are compact and well arched, with tough pads.

The dachshund has five toes on each front foot, only four of which are in use. They are close together, with a pronounced arch, strong nails and tough toe-pads.

The trunk should have high, long withers and follow a straight line, arching slightly in the area of the loins. The breastbone is strong and so prominent that a depression appears on either side. Viewed from the front, the chest appears oval; full-volumed, its ample capacity allows for complete development of heart and lungs. It is well ribbed up and merges gradually into the line of the abdomen. The abdomen should be slightly drawn up.

The hindquarters: Viewed from behind, a well-muscled, long, round, broad rump is seen; pelvic bones not too short, strongly developed, and moderately sloping. The thigh bones should be sturdy and of good length, the hind legs well rounded, the knee joints broad and strong. In comparison with other breeds of dogs, the lower legs (calf bones) are short. They are perpendicular to the thigh bones and are firmly muscled. The tarsal bones are wide set; the hock is strongly prominent. The metatarsus is long, movable toward the

Glossary for Dachshund Owners

Pendant Ears:	The hanging ears.
Blaze:	Marks different color at certain places on the body.
Dappled (sable):	Spots of different colors on the coat.
Dry:	The skin lies on top of connective tissue that is low in fat; the contours of the bones and tendons are discernible.
Feathers:	Fringes of hair on the front and back legs in longhaired dachshunds.
Glassy eye:	Light-colored eye caused by lack of pigment in iris.
Leathery ends:	Short hairs on the lower edges of the ears.
Mutation:	Sudden change in genetic makeup.
Muzzle:	The head in front of the eyes; the mouth and the jaws.
Plume:	The long hairs on the underside of the tail in longhaired dachshunds.
Rudder:	The tail.
Sable:	Black stripes over the ground color.
Standard:	Description of the ideal type of a breed with all its characteristics.
Tattooing:	Marking a dog by inscribing a number in its ear.

These two puppies are frolicking exuberantly. Their toy—a rawhide ball—has been completely forgotten in their great enthusiasm. While playing, young dogs experiment with modes of behavior that are important in later life.

calf bone and slightly bent toward the front. The hind paws have four compactly closed and beautifully arched toes, as in the case of the front paws. The dog should walk on the entire foot, including the footpads, not merely on the toes. The nails are short and sturdy. Viewed from behind, the hindquarters should appear completely straight.

The tail should be a continuation of the spine; it should taper the tip without any pronounced curvature.

Tip: If you are interested in all the details of the official breed characteristics, you can order a free brochure entitled "The Official Standard for the Dachshund" from the American Kennel Club (for address, see page 63).

Coat Color, Nose, Nails

One-colored dachshunds have red (tan) or reddish yellow hair, with or without interspersed short, stubby black hairs. A pure color is preferable; red is considered more desirable than reddish yellow. Dachshunds with a high proportion of interspersed black hairs also are classified as one-colored. The nose and nails are black.

In two-colored dachshunds the coat is deep black, chocolate, gray, or white, always with reddish yellow markings (blaze) above the eyes, on the sides of the jaw and underlip, on the inner edge of the ears, on the chest, on the inside and back of the legs, on the paws, around the anus, and from there to about one-third to one-half the length of the underside of the tail. The nose and nails are black in black dogs; brown or black in chocolate dogs, and gray or even flesh color in gray or white dogs. (Flesh-colored nose and nails, however, are not desirable in terms of the breed standard.) In one-colored and not exactly white two-colored dachshunds, a white nose and nails are not desirable. But small spots or patches are admissible.

Dappled (sable) dachshunds: The hair color of a dappled dachshund is a light, brownish, grayish, or even white ground with dark, irregular patches (large patches are not desirable) that are dark gray, brown, reddish yellow, or black. Neither the light nor the dark color should predominate. Sable dachshunds are red with lacings of dark hairs. Nose and nails are the same as in one-colored and two-colored dachshunds.

Dachshunds of other colors may display any color not mentioned previously. These are considered faults: black or white color without long ears. A blaze that is too broad or too indistinctly demarcated is not desirable.

Special Features of the Various Types

In addition to appropriate physical characteristics, the three varieties of dachshunds:

- shorthaired
- wirehaired
- longhaired.

must display certain properties unique to each variety:

Shorthaired (Smooth) Dachshunds

The coat should be short, thick, shiny, and smooth. No bald patches should be evident anywhere on the body. Other faults are overly fine, thin hair, leathery ends on the long ears, hairless places on the bridge of the nose, and too coarse or too abundant hair in general. The tail should taper gradually to a point and be well, but not too abundantly, covered with hair. Slightly longer straight hair on the underside of the tail is not considered a fault, but an indication of a hereditary heavy growth

Leashes that roll up automatically and are equipped with a push-button braking device are handy (top). They allow a dog a radius of movement of about 16.5 feet (5 m). Also recommended for dachshunds are shoulder leashes that include a collar with a choke ring (above).

of hair. (A brush tail, however, is a fault, as is a partially or completely hairless tail.)

Wirehaired Dachshunds

Except for the muzzle, eyebrows, and ears, the entire body is covered with a completely uniform, close-fitting, dense, wiry coat, interspersed with finer, shorter hairs (undercoat). A beard should grow on the chin. The eyebrows are bushy. The hair on the ears is shorter than on the body, almost smooth, but in keeping with the rest of the hair. The tail hair should be coarse, but as close-fitting as possible, and it should taper without a brush. The overall appearance of the hair should be such that the wirehaired dachshund, when seen from a distance, looks like the shorthaired variety. The following are considered faults: hair that is soft or long and sticks out in all directions from the body; curly or wavy hair; a plume tail. Short hair without a beard and eyebrows is as much of a fault as clipped hair.

Longhaired Dachshunds

Longhaired dachshunds differ from the shorthaired variety in only one respect: their longer, silky hair. The soft, straight, shiny hair grows longer under the neck, on the entire underside of the body, and especially on the ears and the backs of the legs, where it forms "feathers." It is longest on the underside of the tail. The hair should extend beyond the lower edge of the ears. Short hair in that area—so-called leathery ends—is undesirable. Too much hair on the paws (known as "mops") is unattractive and a hindrance in hunting. The tail is carried as a graceful extension of the line formed by the spine. The body hair is longest there

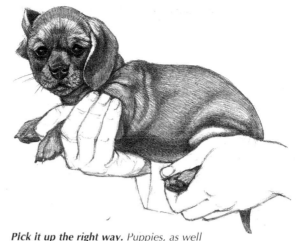

Pick it up the right way. *Puppies, as well as fully grown dogs, should be picked up and carried as follows: Place one hand under the dog's front paws and the other, for proper support, beneath its rear end.*

and forms a perfect plume. It is a fault if the dog has hair—that is, if it is uniformly hairy over its entire body. Other faults include excessively curly, wavy, or shaggy hair, the lack of a plume, the absence of overhanging hair on the ears, a pronounced parting in the hair on the back, and overly long hair between the toes.

Before You Buy a Dachsund

For Would-be Buyers: Examine Your Conscience

Unfortunately, feeling love for a dog is not a sufficient guarantee that you will also give your pet appropriate living conditions. Keeping a dog is extremely time-consuming and entails numerous chores and financial expenditures. For these reasons, before buying a dog, ask yourself a few basic questions:

1. A dachshund may live to be 10 to 15 years old. Are you ready and able to devote two to three hours per day to your dog? That includes at least one fairly long walk every day.
2. The dog should never be left alone for more than four hours. Can your family make the appropriate arrangements?
3. Are you aware that a puppy, like a small child, needs constant supervision?
4. Do you have someone to take care of the dog when you are ill or away on a trip?
5. Year after year, a dog will put you to considerable expense for equipment and accessories, food, veterinary bills, license, and possibly liability insurance. Can you handle these expenses?
6. Does your landlord or your condominium association allow you to keep a pet in your home? This question absolutely must be answered before you buy a dog. Be sure to get permission in writing to keep the dog.
7. Is any member of your family allergic to dog hair? If in doubt, consult your doctor before acquiring a dog.

Before you acquire a dachshund, ask yourself seriously whether you can provide the dog with a happy life. Keeping a dog not only entails expense, but also requires two to three hours of your time every day.

What Can a Purebred Offer?

If you buy a purebred dog, you associate certain things with that label. Not only is the animal's external appearance known beyond all doubt, but you also know what special abilities and what traits of character to expect. The dachshund, which, after all, was bred for centuries as a hunting dog, still possesses the traits of a hunting dog. It is self-confident and courageous, and subsequently strong willed. Moreover, as an old hunter, it naturally pursues every scent that it picks up.

Some people, however, are more interested in the dog, simply as a friendly household companion, than in the pedigree of the animal. Mixed-breeds are said to be possibly smarter, healthier, and better-natured than selectively bred pedigreed dogs. Still, in this case, it would be advisable to find out all you can about the parents of the dog, in order to rule out unpleasant surprises.

A Male or a Female?

The widespread opinion that females are more affectionate and loyal, while males are easier to keep, is not one I can confirm from my long years of experience with both genders. The facts are as follows:

Females

A female dog, or bitch, goes into heat every six months, and during this time she is able to conceive young. If you want to prevent a dog from becoming

At full speed, this wirehaired dachshund runs after the ball that its mistress has thrown for it.

pregnant, you can choose one of several methods of contraception available today:

Hormone treatment administered by a veterinarian to suppress heat, or estrus, is possible but not recommended, because inflammation of the uterus frequently results.

Sterilization—that is, tubal ligation—does prevent fertilization, but does not eliminate all the side effects of estrus and false pregnancy. For that reason it is not recommended.

Spaying is the best solution. This is the term used for removal of a female dog's ovaries and uterus. This operation will not impair her health; on the contrary, it is a way to guard against diseases of the uterus due to age and to prevent pseudopregnancies. The dog will lead a less stressful life. Be sure to feed her slightly less, because after spaying she will tend to put on some weight.

Before your little dachshund comes to live with you, you need to have on hand all the essentials for its care and grooming. Then you can devote yourself unreservedly to your new house companion as it explores its new domain.

Shopping List

Buy the following items for your pet:

- one food dish and one water bowl;
- puppy food;
- a basket or crate lined with a washable blanket;
- leash and collar;
- toys;
- comb and brush;
- capsule or name tag address.

Once the dog has taken up residence in your home, it also needs these:

- vaccination record;
- license from local municipality in which your dog will be living.

What a Dachshund Needs Every Day

A Place to Sleep

Drawing 1

The dog wants its own place to be arranged so that it feels safe and protected there.

Location: It is important that the spot be chosen with some deliberation. Look for a quiet, draft-free location. The dog needs as good a vantage point as possible, so that it can observe everything that goes on and participate in life around it. It will also learn a great deal by observing. Nevertheless, at times, it also

has to be able to withdraw and be undisturbed. Young dogs need plenty of sleep. If the puppy's basket stands in a spot with a great deal of through traffic, the commotion and the animal's own curiosity will rouse it from its slumber and continually encourage it to leave its place.

Igloo: Small dogs like dachshunds like having a roof over their heads. Pet stores sell so-called dog igloos in various styles.

Baskets: They look attractive, but for small dachshunds in particular they are a great temptation to try out their little teeth.

Crate: At the beginning, you also could fix up an appropriate crate—with a front opening—for use as a dog bed.

Food Dish and Water Bowl

Drawing 2

Your dog needs a bowl in which fresh water is always available and a food dish. These containers should be made of a material that is easy to clean, can't be gnawed, and won't slide around on your floor. Good examples would be a water bowl of glazed clay and a food dish made of high-grade stainless steel, with a skid-proof rubber rim on the bottom.

Collar

For a young dachshund, a simple leather collar is sufficient, as the dog will outgrow it anyway after a few months. You can also choose a simple type of leash. The mature dachshund will need a sturdy collar and an equally

1. A bed made of wicker is both suitable and attractive. Many puppies, however, like to test their teeth on the wicker.

2. *Food dishes made of high-grade steel are easy to clean.*

strong leash. Good choices are shoulder leashes, so-called guide leashes, which include a collar with a choke ring. They are for training dachshunds and for using them in hunting, but they are also excellent for everyday use. Many owners also like to use plastic leashes that roll up automatically. Pet stores offer a large selection of them. Heavy leather or chain collars are not suitable for dachshunds. At no time should you put a harness on your dachshund. It absolutely does not conform to a dachshund's anatomy and could even cause health problems.

Brush and Comb
Drawing 3
A brush with natural bristles is best. From the beginning, your little dachshund needs to get used to daily brushing; it feels good and is healthful as well. A flea comb with very close-set teeth should also be part of your pet's equipment.

Toys
Drawing 4
Don't forget toys; they are important for young dogs, that want—and need—to use their teeth. A great many kinds of toys are available, but be aware that not all of them are safe for a young dachshund.

Suitable toys are made from rawhide or in the form of solid rubber balls and rings. They can be chewed as much as the dog likes and still stand up well to its little teeth without causing any harm to the dog. The same is true of rawhide toys.

Unsuitable toys, on the other hand, are any made of plastic or wood. Here there is a danger that the young dog will bite off pieces of them and perhaps swallow them. Squeaking toys also are gnawed apart very quickly by many dogs.

Moreover, the metal squeaker can be swallowed. It is not advisable to give a young dog an old shoe as a plaything. How will the little creature learn later on to distinguish between "old" and "still in use"? The same applies to paper. Dachshunds really are incapable of telling the difference between today's newspaper and yesterday's, nor do they know whether the paper they pick up off the hall floor is a letter that the postal carrier has put through the slot or just some unimportant sheet of paper.

Feeding Puppies
To avoid major difficulties in adjusting, ask the previous owner what the dog was being fed. If you don't want to prepare the food yourself, you also can get special commercial puppy feed from pet stores.

3. *A brush and a fine-toothed comb are essential for grooming your pet's fur. If you have a longhaired dachshund, you need a coarse-toothed comb as well.*

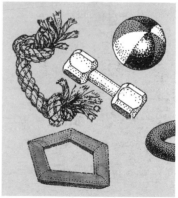

4. *Toys made of solid rubber or rawhide are highly recommended. Puppies also enjoy pulling pieces of heavy, natural-colored rope all around the house.*

A leap into the cool water was the only way this dachshund could reach the island.

Males

They are always ready for romance as soon as a female dog in heat appears in their neighborhood.

Neutering—removal of the testicles—is uncalled for if your male's behavior is otherwise calm and steady. The following behaviors are indications that you should consider neutering your pet:

- increased readiness to get into scraps with other male dogs;
- tendency to stray and run away;
- if the male suffers so greatly from his unfulfilled drives that he almost stops eating and loses weight.

Where to Get Your Dog

Buying a dog is a matter of confidence. For this reason, buy your dog only where you can be sure that you are getting good advice.

The following are places where you can safely buy a dog:

Reputable pet stores. The pet store owner should not offer dogs for sale in the display window; instead he should advise you and help you obtain a dog.

Breeders: Addresses are available from the American Dachshund Club and the American Kennel Club (for addresses, see page 63). There you can obtain, free of charge, the addresses of small-scale breeders near you and learn the current market prices of dachshunds.

Hobby breeders and dog owners who are not connected with any organization. The puppies usually are advertised for sale in the daily newspapers under the heading "Animals for Sale." Read the ads with a critical eye!

Animal shelters and private organizations for the prevention of cruelty to animals. Looking for a dog here is a praiseworthy decision. Keep in mind, however, that the longer a dog has lived in a shelter and the older it is, the more problematic its behavior can be. Here you need a great deal of experience with dogs.

Don't buy your dachshund from a so-called large-scale breeder or "puppy mill" who produces all possible breeds of dogs. The health and disposition of these puppies are frequently unsatisfactory.

How to Choose Your Puppy

In selecting a puppy, don't let yourself be guided by your feelings; ask yourself these questions:

Where and how is the puppy going to grow up? Behavioral research tells us that the first 12 weeks are decisive in the formation of a dog's character. If a puppy has spent the entire time in a cage and has had little or even poor contact with humans, it will later encounter them with great caution and mistrust.

If you want a family pet, make sure that the dog has been reared from birth in a family with children and visitors.

That way it has had a chance to get used to the noise level common in daily family life.

Don't delay: Pick out your puppy early. Visit the mother and her pups frequently, to see how the little dogs are developing.

Watch closely: While playing, the puppies will reveal a great deal about their character and predisposition. If you watch them quietly, you soon can tell which is the leader of the pack and which keeps to itself, tends to be cautious, or even stays out of the games altogether.

Decide now: The older the puppies get, the more clearly their differences in character and in physical appearance will stand out.

Depending on your expectations, you will decide either on a dachshund with a great capacity for getting its own way (later it will put this ability to the test in dealing with you) or one that is more compliant and therefore easier to train.

How to Tell a Healthy Puppy

To enable you to judge the state of your future housemate's health, here are a few attributes that you should by all means look for:

- thick, glossy coat, free from parasites;
- clear eyes with no sign of inflammation;
- clean ears without any redness or sticky matter;
- body neither too thin nor too fat—it is all right for the puppy to have a plump little tummy.

The well-known phenomenon of "love at first sight" also occurs between humans and dogs. However, don't let that feeling alone guide you when you decide on a dachshund puppy. Observe the baby dachshund carefully, as puppies reveal a great deal about their disposition when they are at play.

Dog Liability Insurance Policy

A liability insurance policy is always useful when the risk connected with the animal has become a reality. The dog that suddenly runs across the street and causes an accident is insured, as is the dog that starts a fight with another dog or pulls a bicycle rider off a bike. As a rule, however, insurance does not cover a dog that is misused as a weapon and employed wittingly and purposefully against humans. Then it is not the risk connected with the animal that materializes, but the imposed will of a human being. For insurance information see page 63.

Dogs in Rented Apartments and Condominiums: What Are the Owner's Rights and Duties with Respect to the Neighbors?

You will search in vain through our many laws for a special legal provision covering this issue. Whether a dog is allowed in a rented apartment or condominium or not depends first on the rental contract and then on the decision of the condominium committee.

In contrast to small animals (canaries, hamsters), keeping dogs in an apartment is not absolutely safe as far as the rules governing tenancy are concerned. If keeping an animal is fundamentally prohibited in the rental contract, you can scarcely get around this ban. This prohibition is operative and entitles the lessor to terminate the lease without notice, if necessary.

The matter is judged differently if the rental or condominium contract specifies that keeping a dog is contingent on the permission of the landlord or condominium owners'committee. The jurisprudence on these problems currently can be summarized in this way: "Dog with good manners allowed." That is, the right of the tenant to keep a dog that does not actually bother the other tenants does not constitute a use of the rental apartment contrary to the terms of the contract, not even if the rental contract specifies that a dog may be kept only with the lessor's permission. Rather, it has to be proved in each individual case that the keeping of a dog does in fact represent an unreasonable nuisance for the other inhabitants of the building..

Tip: Life in a community is based on mutual consideration, and dog-loving tenants living in a community have the right to expect consideration for their fondness of animals. However, dog owners should also take into consideration the need of their fellow tenants for peace and quiet. You should give both the lessor and the neighbors advance notice of your intention to keep a dog.

In the case of an owner-occupied apartment, a general prohibition against keeping a dog fundamentally cannot be adopted. What is usually permissible, however, is a decision by all the owners to the effect that the keeping of pets in owner-occupied apartments is to be restricted to a reasonable number of animals. Thus, for example, the right to limit an owner to one dog and one cat is usually conceded.

What Is the Dog Owner Liable for? Who Is Liable If Children Are Out with the Dog?

Many local laws stipulate that the animal's owner in principle is liable if a person is killed or injured or anything is damaged by an animal. In this regard, we speak of a so-called "endangerment liability." That means that dog owners are always liable when a voluntary behavior of their dog in accordance with its typical nature was the cause. Such behaviors include biting and hunting.

Tip: Even with a well-trained dog, it is not completely impossible for the animal to enforce its own will and thereby cause damage. Liability insurance for dog owners, therefore, is a good idea if you or members of your family want to avoid paying for any such damage claims.

When and How Long May a Dog Bark Indoors or in the Yard?

If neighbors feel that dogs are causing such a racket that the normal sound level is exceeded, they can demand forbearance from the dog's owner and, if necessary, can even achieve that objective by legal means. This holds true even when a watchdog is being kept. Courts have decided that the barking of an animal always infringes on the neighbor's legal status as a property owner; it is immaterial whether the dog's barking exceeds a certain sound level. Noises that attract attention are always irritating infringements,

even if they do not exceed the sound level at which even traffic and industrial noises are still tolerable.

Is There a Federal or State Law That Dogs May Not Dirty the Street, or Is This a Community Issue?

Most cities have "pooper scooper" laws. Dog excrement shouldn't be left on the sidewalk, but this call of nature cannot always be avoided. Fines for the person walking the dog can result, as authorities have affirmed that a danger to public health exists when sidewalks are soiled by dogs relieving themselves. This is based on the medically substantiated fact that dogs can carry certain diseases. Moreover, the dirtying of sidewalks by dog excrement also presents a threat insofar as it can result in pedestrians' slipping and possibly injuring themselves. Even worse, if you let your dog deposit its excrement on a playground with a grassy area or in a grassy area used for sunbathing, and fail to remove it, this constitutes a breach of regulations, perhaps even a statutory offense—failure to remove ecologically hazardous waste in accordance with the law.

Tip: To remove the dog excrement, handy disposable scoops

for dog droppings (available in pet stores), small shovels, paper towels, and plastic bags can be used.

Care and Grooming

Acclimating a Puppy

When a little puppy leaves its mother and brothers and sisters for a new environment, it faces a big change. Too loud or too stormy a welcome by friends or children could frighten the young dog. At first, give it plenty of time to sniff everything and explore its new home. Show the puppy where it is to sleep and eat (see How To: Equipment and Accessories, pages 14–15) and, little by little, visit the other rooms. If it gets something to eat once the initial excitement dies down, it will immediately feel safer and more secure in its new family. Then, once it has been taken outdoors to do its business, let it rest in its new sleeping spot. The initial adjustment period should be calm, with an opportunity for the little dog to get used to its new surroundings and the daily routine in its new family.

The First Training Problem: Staying Alone

The first problem arises the evening after the puppy's arrival in its new family. It is used to being constantly in the company of its mother and siblings, but now it is suddenly supposed to spend the night all alone in its little basket. This is quite difficult for the dog, a pack animal, and only a few dogs

Billy scratches his wirehaired dachshund.
A dachshund and a child can become friends, provided the dog has had no bad experiences with children.

accept it without a more or less noisy protest.

Various methods can help ease the adjustment:

At night you can put the basket containing the dog next to your bed, so that the little animal can sense that another living being is nearby. If it still whimpers, it can be comforted by stroking or by soothing words.
The drawback of this method is that being alone will remain an unfamiliar experience for the puppy. Then, if you have to leave it alone during the day, its protests will be even more vociferous.

A tougher method: Bring the dog and its basket into a room where the animal can't do any damage. Go to it only when its whimpering grows too loud; pet it briefly until it has calmed down.

Most younger dogs very quickly resign themselves to their altered situation and cease their "protest songs."

If you live in an apartment building, it is advisable to explain the circumstances to your neighbors and ask for a little indulgence in case the dog cries for a few nights. Hopefully, they will be understanding!

During the day, get the little dog used to being alone. Put the dachshund—with its basket, of course, and if possible with a toy—for a short time in a safe room (for example, the kitchen or the bathroom). If it starts to whimper or howl, scold it and send it to its basket. Alternatively, take no notice of it at all.

Appropriate living conditions, loving care, and attention are the major prerequisites for keeping your dog healthy and able to engage in its natural modes of behavior.

At first, leave it alone for only 15 minutes, longer if it keeps quiet. Let it out only if it is really still and doesn't fuss too much! Otherwise, it will think: "All I have to do is cry as loudly as I can, and then I'll be taken out of here again!"

How to Housebreak a Dachshund

If this training objective is to be met in the first two or three weeks, you will have to constantly keep an eye on your little puppy, because its behavior will give you advance notice of its need. That takes a lot of time, patience, and firmness, but it pays off.

Obvious Signs

If, while playing the dog suddenly lowers its head and starts sniffing around, the utmost haste is called for. If it begins to whimper at night in its basket, that is also an unmistakable indication.

Take It Outside Regularly

It is important to take the dog outside regularly—during the first few days, every two to three hours. The puppy has to learn that it can go outside at set intervals—and that it will be showered with praise there if it does its business.

After Waking Up and Eating

A little dog always has to relieve itself when it wakes up or when it has just eaten. Immediately after naps and meals, always take it to the same spot—wherever it is you want it to relieve itself. Praise the dog if it is successful.

A Designated Spot

Puppies need to get used to a certain spot where they are allowed to relieve themselves. Find a little place near home where the dog can do its business in peace and quiet, without becoming a public nuisance. You will have to remove any dog excrement deposited on the sidewalk, and remember that children's playgrounds and

This easily inserted, burglarproof grating for car windows has the advantage of letting your pet enjoy fresh air if it has to wait in the car.

sandboxes are taboo. Granted, in a large city it's not easy to find a suitable "dog potty." You will save yourself a great deal of trouble and enmity, however, if you are considerate of your fellow human beings where your dog's bowel movements are concerned.

A Special Case: The "Indoor Potty"

If you keep your dog in an upstairs apartment or in a high-rise building, it's not always possible to take it outside right away. People in this situation have found ways to set up a permanent toilet area, furnished with newspaper. When you think the little dog needs to relieve itself, set it on the paper and praise it if it does so.

In addition, take it outside regularly. Take the newspaper along, put it on a patch of grass, and praise the dog if it does something. In this way, you can keep it from making a habit of the indoor toilet.

If an Accident Happens

If the dog persists in doing its business indoors in the wrong place, saying "Phooey" or something similar in a sharp tone of voice will help only if done immediately after the dog's misdeed and if you catch it in the act. A loud tongue-lashing or even punishment only frightens the animal. And makes the task of housebreaking more difficult.

Clean the spot with a disinfectant or a mixture of vinegar and water to keep your dog from sniffing out that place and returning to it.

Suddenly Developing Problems

Once your dog is housebroken, it usually will remain so. Consequently, you need to look for the reasons that cause the dog to suddenly relieve itself in "forbidden" places. If the veterinarian has ruled out any physical illness, it might be that an emotional problem has unsettled the animal. Have any changes occurred in your family? Have you moved? Could the dog be jealous of a new baby or another pet in the family? Do you have less time available to spend with your pet? In these and similar situations, you can usually help your dog by showing it more affection and patience.

Daily Care: Brushing the Coat

The most important type of grooming for all three coat types is daily brushing. First brush against the lie of the hair, then with it. That does more than clean the fur; it also is a soothing massage that simultaneously helps the dog's circulation.

Shorthaired dachshunds require the least grooming, because almost nothing can cling to their short fur. Regular brushing is enough.

With wirehaired dachshunds, the dull, dead hair has to be plucked out in the spring and fall, after molting. The procedure will cause your dog no pain, because this hair has no roots.

With longhaired dachshunds, however, the long, silky hair needs to be combed through again after thorough brushing. Mats, which develop primarily behind the ears and in areas where the hair is longer, are best untangled by hand. Only in very extreme cases should you cut off the matted hair.

Seeds of all kinds from woods and fields tend to get caught in the dog's fur. There is a danger that the seeds will travel from the ears into the ear canal and cause inflammation there (see Ears, page 26). After every walk through fields and woods, you need to remove these annoying little souvenirs from your pet. That is best done with a dust comb. Be sure to check the insides of the long ears with special care.

Burrs are also a great nuisance. They can get so matted in the hairs on the dog's chest, abdomen, and legs that the animal is reluctant to keep walking. To prevent that, I always carry a small pair of scissors with me, so that I can remove the burrs as quickly and safely as possible.

Tip: Additional grooming procedures that are necessary at certain intervals are found on pages 26–27, in the How-To section on grooming.

Traveling with Your Dachshund

Basically, you can take your dachshund along almost everywhere you go—you just have to slowly get it used to certain situations, such as riding in the car or walking in the city.

In Town

In a city, always put your dog on its leash, regardless of whether it is accus-

Marking. *It is primarily males that mark their territory by lifting a leg and releasing a few drops of urine. In this way they mask the scent of any dog that has been there before them.*

These two smooth-coated dachshunds don't pass up any opportunity to take a refreshing dip.

tomed to city life or is only there on a visit. It might be startled by a vehicle, or something might suddenly arouse its hunting instinct—causing it to run like mad. These unanticipated reactions are particularly dangerous in a city.

Equipment for removing dog excrement (disposable scoop, paper towels, and paper or plastic bag) should always be brought along. Leaving dog droppings on the sidewalk is not only inconsiderate of others, but also punishable by fine in many cities.

Tip: Sets for removing dog excrement are available in pet stores.

In the Car

Your dog needs its own permanent place in the car. For little dogs, the best place is up front on the floor mat, right in front of the passenger seat. While

the car is moving, don't let your pet ride with its head out of an open window! Serious eye and ear inflammations can result. On longer trips, be sure to take breaks regularly, so that the dog can get some exercise and relieve itself. Don't forget to give it fresh water from time to time. In summer, when temperatures are high, leave your dog alone in the car only in an emergency, and then only for a brief time. Always leave one window open, so that the dog has enough fresh air. Pet stores carry burglarproof window grating (see drawing, page 22).

Make it a habit to always put your dog on a leash before you get out of the car. Many a poor dachshund, happy to regain its freedom, has bolted from the car right under the wheels of another vehicle.

Motion sickness affects primarily young dachshunds. Your veterinarian can prescribe medication to prevent nausea in your dog. However, I have used a different method with success: gradually getting the dog used to riding in a car. For it to work, two people with time and patience are needed: the driver and one other person. Quiet streets are also essential, because you will have to stop frequently and as quickly as possible at the side of the road. The non-driver needs to watch the dachshund carefully, as it almost always will indicate that it is about to get sick.

Heavy panting, nervous licking, and general restlessness are signs that it is time to stop the car. Quickly get out with your dog—on its leash, of course—let it sniff and perhaps relieve itself. It will be distracted, regain its equilibrium and feel better.

Repeat this routine several times.

Vacation Travel

You can take your dachshund to almost every country in the world, if you adhere to the stipulated quarantine regulations. Exceptions are England, Ireland, Sweden, Norway, and Finland, and the state of Hawaii, because they require a quarantine period of several months.

Papers: Almost all countries ask to see proof of vaccination against rabies upon entry, and some also require an official veterinary medical certificate. Ask your veterinarian or, when in doubt, inquire at the appropriate consulate to learn what rules apply.

Public transportation: For a well-trained dog, using public transportation presents no problem. Inquire at each specific office (railway, airline, or shipping company) or ask your travel agent what regulations govern your pet's trav-el. When traveling by air, for example, you need to find out whether the dog may fly in the passenger cabin or in the cargo compartment. A special carrier is required in either case. (See drawing, page 54.)

Portable medicine case: When you are getting your own medicine case ready, give some thought to your pet's needs as well. The following items often prove useful for dogs: bandaging materials, wound ointment, flea spray, medication to treat diarrhea, and a laxative to relieve constipation. Your veterinarian can provide these products and will explain their use.

Tip: During the trip, don't let your dog have much to eat; the dachshund is not going to starve to death on the spot. However, you do need to remember that a supply of fresh water is crucial to your pet's health.

HOW-TO:
Grooming

Because a dachshund should not be clipped or trimmed, its grooming is relatively simple and costs very little. You can perform almost all the procedures yourself.

Checking the Ears
Drawing 1

Frequent scratching and head-shaking may be symptomatic of an inflammation or a foreign object in the dog's ears. Ears that are severely reddened or that extrude blackish brown, purulent, or even bloody matter must be treated by a veterinarian. Such problems can be largely prevented by regularly checking and cleaning the ears. Once a week, clean your dachshund's ears with one of the liquid ear-cleaning preparations available in pet stores. With an eyedropper, put a few drops of the liquid into the

1. Wipe out the ears with a paper tissue twisted into a point.

projecting outer portion of the ear, then rub it in well. Finally, when the earwax or dirt have become loosened, carefully clean the ears again, using a paper tissue twisted to form a point.

Dental Care
Drawing 2

Once a week, you can clean the dog's teeth with a special toothpaste (available at veterinary clinics and in pet stores). Check the teeth regularly for plaque. Any plaque buildup should be removed by a veterinarian. Plaque formation can be prevented by proper nutrition.

As a counterbalance to soft dog food, give your dachshund something hard to bite as well, like rawhide bones. The mechanical abrasion of the teeth inhibits plaque buildup. To prevent malocclusion, pay close attention as the growing dachshund gets its second set of teeth, between the fifth and seventh months of life. In small dachshunds, in particular, the first fangs—also called canine teeth—often do not fall out on their own. The other fangs then grow behind the "milk teeth," which are still firmly in place. Gnawing on a veal bone often works miracles in such cases! If that fails, the veterinarian will have to extract the milk teeth.

Baths—But Not Too Often

All dachshunds need about two years for their coats to mature thoroughly. A dachshund's skin, especially when the dog is still developing, produces a special

hair fat that serves as an insulating layer to protect against all types of weather factors—sun, rain, snow, and icy cold. The more frequently you bathe your pet with dog shampoo, the softer its coat of hair becomes.

As a rule, rinsing your dog off with clear, lukewarm water is sufficient to get it clean. Remember that thorough brushing also cleans the dog. If a real bath does become necessary, use a special dog shampoo. When you rinse the shampoo out, make sure to cover the dog's eyes with your hand. To ward off a chill, rub the dog dry, then let its fur dry completely in a warm room, or blow-dry it.

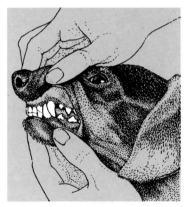

2. Checking the teeth: Carefully pull upward and downward on the dog's chops (flews).

Paws

Especially during the cold months of the year, the dachshund's coat can grow quickly and form so-called "mops." Dogs that get their exercise predominantly on soft grass and forest soil do not wear down the hairs between the pads of their feet. These long hairs have to be trimmed and cut out from between the pads, to keep clumps of ice or dirt from forming there in winter or damp weather. These little clumps can often cause a dachshund so much pain that it simply does not want to walk.

Pads and Nails

Ice, snow, and thawing salt can cause a great deal of trouble for your dachshund's paws. Before taking a walk in winter, carefully rub the pads with a rich skin cream. Overly long nails can impair the dog's ability to walk and can cause painful changes in the posture of the paws. For that reason, from time to time you need to trim any nails that are too long. Do so with great care, to keep from injuring the "quick"—the tender, sensitive portion of the nails through which blood flows. Alternatively, your veterinarian can shorten overgrown nails.

Eye Care
Drawing 3

Small bits of matter can build up in the corners of a dog's eyes while it sleeps. Gently remove this eye discharge with a damp, lint-free cloth or a cotton swab.

Removing Pests
Drawing 4

Even the best-groomed dog may come home one day with pests. You need to check your dachshund regularly for such

pests, so that you can remove them without delay. Your pet will indicate by restlessness and frequent scratching that it is plagued by skin parasites. You can use a dust comb, also known as a flea comb, to examine your pet's fur.

Fleas are present all year long. If you find some on your dog, you can choose among various controls: powders, shampoos, and sprays. When using one of them, it is important that the dog's sleeping place and blanket, as well as the surroundings—including baseboards and carpet—be given the same treatment.

The entire treatment should be repeated within one week,

3. With a cotton swab, carefully remove any eye discharge.

because new fleas can hatch from the undestroyed flea eggs. Fleas can serve as an intermediate host for tapeworms, so a dog that has fleas also should be wormed!

The period from early June to mid-September is high season

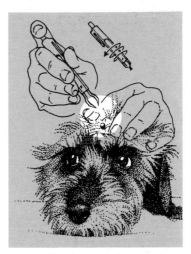

4. Put a few drops of oil on the tick and twist it out with special tick tweezers.

for ticks. They can give your dog borreliosis (Lyme Disease), a skin and joint disease. If a tick is firmly lodged, dab it with some cooking oil or baby oil. Wait a bit to let the oil take effect, then turn the tick until it comes off. That is best done with special tick tweezers, available in pet stores. When you remove the tick, don't leave the head behind; inflammation can result!

To safeguard your dog against additional infestations of parasites, have it wear an antiparasite collar (available in pet stores).

Proper Nutrition

We are what we eat—that maxim holds true for both humans and their pets. For your dachshund's growth, for its well-being and the maintenance of its health—particularly in old age—it is essential that you feed it properly; or should I say, appropriately.

An Appropriate Diet

Although dogs are carnivores, they cannot live on a diet of muscle meats alone. Their organs resemble those of their ancestors, the wolves, and are adapted to digest and utilize plant-eating small animals. Their quarries are devoured to the last morsel, including the tendons, ligaments, and bones. The stomach and entrails of the victim contain undigested chyme, which consists largely of plant substances. In this way, a dog's body gets roughage, protein, carbohydrates, fats, minerals like calcium and phosphorus, vitamins, and trace elements.

Commercial Dog Foods

Commercial dog food has many advantages: It is quick and easy to prepare, and it contains everything your dachshund needs. An entire team of specialists makes sure that the mixture is prepared in accordance with the findings of nutritional science.

Moist or canned dog food (water content: 75 percent) is the type most commonly used to feed dogs. It is a complete food, containing all necessary nutrients and anabolic substances. Pet food companies offer two types of canned foods:

A healthful diet is just as important for dachshunds as for humans. If you think you're showing special love for your pet by slipping it tidbits constantly, you're in serious error. On the contrary, your dog will get too fat and may develop life-threatening diseases.

One that contains mainly meat and/or raw materials that are protein sources (muscle meat, tripe, heart, liver, and lungs).

The second kind is enriched with carbohydrates in the form of grains (rice, barley, oats, wheat, or corn).

You should give preference to canned dog foods with few chemical additives. To keep your dog's teeth and gums healthy, give it something hard to bite— veal gristle or bones—in addition to the soft canned dog food (see page 30).

Semimoist dog food (moisture content: 25 to 30 percent) and dry food (moisture content: 10 to 20 percent) are, in comparison with canned dog foods, much more concentrated and therefore supply considerably more energy. The moisture removed from the food has to be replaced by a commensurate intake of fluids. Make sure your dog has an ample supply of fresh drinking water. Dry dog food can also be softened in vegetables, broth made from bones, or water.

How to Use Commercial Dog Foods

When feeding your pet commercial dog foods, follow these rules:

- To keep the dog from having diarrhea, always mix canned dog food with meal or kibble (⅔ moist food, ⅓ admixture of meal and vegetable combinations).
- If you serve canned dog food straight from the refrigerator, add hot water to it, or it also can give your dog diarrhea.

Two good friends—the wirehaired dachshund and the smooth-coated dachshund.

- If you use dry dog food, it is very important to be sure that the dachshund has fresh water available.

My Tip: However well balanced commercial dog foods may be, your dog still appreciates variety and will enjoy a meal prepared especially for it. On pages 34 and 35 you will learn how to prepare food at home.

Where and When to Feed Your Pet

When you're eating, you like to enjoy your meal in peace and quiet. Your dog feels the same way; its food and water dishes should stand in a place where the dog can eat undisturbed, a spot that is accessible around the clock, so that it can drink whenever it wishes. Make a rule of observing fixed mealtimes that the dog can get used to. A grown dog (12 months and over) needs its main meal at midday and a small additional portion in the evening. If these mealtimes don't fit your schedule, you can shift the main meal to the morning or early evening. In that case, however, you need to make sure that the dog is taken outside to relieve itself four to six hours after eating.

Drinking Is Important

Fresh water has to be available to your dog at all times. Milk is not a beverage for daily consumption, because in undiluted form it has a laxative effect. Old dogs, in particular, tend to drink too little. If your dog is not drinking enough water, offer it a mixture of skim milk or buttermilk and water in equal parts. However, follow up to see whether your dog suffers from diarrhea as a result.

Bones for Your Dog

To preserve and care for your dog's teeth, it is vital that the dachshund have something to bite. Particularly if its diet is predominantly commercial soft dog food, it needs rawhide chewing bones, hard dog biscuits, or meat-bones as a counterbalance (see drawing on page 43). Do not give bones to your pet more than twice a week. Most suitable are joints of large veal and beef bones, so-called ball joints.

Be careful with poultry and pork bones: The cylindrical flinty hard bones of poultry will splinter and may lead to injuries in the intestinal track. Pork ribs—chops or spare ribs—can be used only in very small quantities. If your dog eats too many of these bones, the result will be constipation, with rock-hard excrement, or, in extreme cases, intestinal obstruction.

Overweight. *Dogs that are too fat commonly suffer from enormous health problems, including joint and disk disease. Only a special diet can help in this case (see page 32).*

Feeding a Young Dog

Young dogs need foods richer in proteins and minerals than mature dogs. Pet stores have special puppy foods available to meet that need. When you get your puppy, it usually is between eight and nine weeks old. Ask the previous owners what the dog has been eating. Have them give you some of the dachshund's food to take home; that will make the adaptation process easier for the little creature. A young dog has to be fed several times a day, according to the following timetable:

- four times a day until the age of three months;
- three times a day until the age of six months;
- thereafter, twice a day.

Feeding an Older Dog

We call a dachshund "old" when it is over 10 years of age. Because its liver, kidneys, and intestines don't function as well in old age, an old dog needs foods high in carbohydrates, which are easier for it to digest. For your dachshund's bill of fare, that means: smaller portions of meat, but more meal or kibble-type dog food, rice, or vegetables.

An Improper Diet Will Make Your Pet Ill

Dachshunds don't have it any easier than many of their masters or mistresses; they have weight problems. Our dogs, however, suffer less from malnutrition and the resulting deficiency symptoms. Their problem is that they get too much of a good thing.

That begins even in early puppyhood. Many breeders, wanting to produce particularly large, powerful dogs, recommend supplying the growing dog with an excess of high-protein and high-energy foods, vitamins, and minerals. The results are disturbances of bone growth and joint diseases. Other dogs are quite simply, too fat. Here's how to determine whether your dog belongs in that category: Feel behind the shoulders, about midway on the chest, to locate the ribs. They should be covered with only a thin layer of fat and should be easily palpable. If you can't feel the ribs, the dog is overweight (see drawing, left page).

Female dogs are generally more apt to overeat than male dogs, but after castration the males are equally inclined to be voracious. Old dogs that don't get much exercise any more also tend to be overweight. They are precisely the ones that should be slim, however, because overweight promotes joint and disk problems in old age. Other consequences of excess weight are an increased burden on the circulatory system and, as a result, inactivity. For these reasons, put your pet on a reducing diet if it is too fat.

A special diet may also be called for if your dog has an allergic reaction to a certain dog food or suffers from an upset stomach. You will find some suggested diet foods on pages 32 and 33. Always keep in mind that you show your dog more love by feeding it appropriately than by plying it with countless tidbits that are not good for it.

Important Feeding Rules

- The dog's meals should be both appropriate and well-balanced.
- Always feed your dog at the same time of day.
- Don't serve your pet leftover dog food.
- The dog needs to rest right after eating.
- Use only hot water to clean the dog's food dish. Detergents or soap don't appeal to a dog's sense of smell.

- Table scraps are not good foods for dogs.
- The dog food should always be served at room temperature.

Amount of Food for Special Diets
- The amount of food depends on the need of the individual dog. It may vary widely from one dog to another, in accordance with the animal's age, amount of exercise, and, above all, ability to utilize the nutrients it eats. Use this as a rough guideline:
- Per day, 8.8 ounces (250 g) for every 22 pounds (10 kg) of the dog's weight.

Note: The type of dog food influences the amount. Canned food is 75–78 percent water; thus, more must be fed than when semimoist or kibble-type dry food is offered.

A Reducing Diet
Primarily, castrated dogs or dogs with hormonal disturbances tend to devour everything in sight; a "garbage chute compulsion." To diminish that urge, give your pet food that is high in fiber.

The puppy watches the hedgehog from a respectful distance.

The ideal recipe:
- 50 percent cooked vegetables of all kinds (except potatoes) as a carbohydrate substitute;
- 25 percent bran, unripe alfalfa meal, or dried beet pulp (available wherever organic produce is sold);
- 25 percent tripe, lean chicken, lamb or veal as meat substitutes;
- 1 teaspoon of vegetable oil per 22 pounds (10 kg) of body weight.

Important: Always feed your dog meat without fat and low-fat dairy products.

Commercial dog foods (dry or canned dog foods) are available in reducing-diet versions from your veterinarian or in pet stores.

An Allergy Diet
The preservatives contained in dry dog foods sometimes trigger food allergies, but even home-prepared food (see pages 34–35) can result in allergies in the form of diarrhea or skin diseases. If that happens, try to feed your pet as bland a diet as possible to determine what is causing the allergic reaction.

The ideal recipe:
- 50 percent lamb, poultry, or farmer cheese; and
- 50 percent rice.

Important: Keep your pet on this diet for one week, until the symptoms disappear. Then, one after another, add the individual components of the diet that triggered the allergy, in order to pinpoint its cause.

Commercial dog foods in allergy diet versions are available from your veterinarian.

A Diet for Dogs with Digestive Problems
Problems in the gastrointestinal area are connected with vomiting and diarrhea. For that reason, you should have

Assembled around the food dish in perfect harmony, these five young dachshunds satisfy their hunger.

the dog fast for a day before starting the special diet. On the fast day, replace your pet's drinking water with small amounts of artificially sweetened black tea. Add it to the dog's water bowl or feed it to the dachshund yourself.

The ingredients of the diet have to be:

- high in carbohydrates (about 70 percent);
- low in protein (about 30 percent); and
- very low in fat.

The ideal recipe:

- 70 percent gruel or rice porridge, with consomme added to improve the taste;

- 30 percent finely chopped cooked lean chicken;
- 1 teaspoon of vegetable oil per 22 pounds (10 kg) of body weight; and
- ½ teaspoon of a liquid vitamin and mineral blend per 22 pounds (10 kg) of body weight, if the diet is followed for an extended period.

Important: Divide the diet food into three or four portions and serve them to the dog spread out over the course of the day. Give your pet only black tea to drink, no water.

Commercial dog foods for animals with digestive problems are available from your veterinarian.

Preparing Tasty Meals for Your Dog

Like humans, dachshunds are delighted when we take the trouble to "cook" for them. Naturally, a meal prepared by you tastes better to your pet than the dog food that comes out of a can or a box.

What the Menu Should Include

To prevent deficiency symptoms, you need to make sure that certain nutritional elements in sufficient quantities are consumed along with the food.

Protein is present primarily in meat, fish, farmer cheese, or cottage cheese, but it is also found in certain plants (soybeans, for example). So-called essential amino acids are found predominantly in animal protein. These acids are small components of the proteins that the body cannot produce itself; they have to be added along with the food.

Since raw meat is relatively hard to digest, you should always give your dog cooked meat. Never feed your pet raw pork, because of the danger of toxoplasmosis and Aujezky's Disease (Pseudorabies). With raw poultry, there is a risk of salmonella.

Carbohydrates are contained chiefly in grain, kibbled dog food, rice, potatoes, corn, and wheat-based products such as noodles, bread, or baked goods. Easy to digest, they contribute essential minerals and vitamins to the body— provided they are made from whole grain.

Fats are contained in meats, particularly in pork. They are the chief suppliers of energy to the body, as they have twice as many calories as carbohydrates and protein. The so-called essential fatty acids are found chiefly in vegetable fats and oils. The body can produce only a part of these acids, so they too must be present in your pet's food.

Minerals, trace elements, and vitamins: These "vital substances" are crucial primarily for young dogs, as well as old or sick animals. They are a component of all the major bodily substances and are found in the blood, bones, muscles, and tissues. They are indispensable for metabolism and the functions of movement.

If you feed your dog kibbled dog food that has been enriched with vitamins, there is no need to add more vitamins to your pet's diet. Blends of vitamins and minerals are available in pet stores or from your veterinarian.

Important: Under no circumstances should you omit any one of the previously listed nutritional building blocks when preparing your pet's meals. It is all right, however, to vary the taste (for example, by choosing fish instead of meat or by seasoning with salt-free garlic or onion powder).

The Ingredients and How to Use Them

I have already described above the nutritional elements that are important parts of a healthy diet for your dachshund. Additional information on the preparation of the ingredients follows:

Meat: It should always be served cooked and chopped into small pieces. These meats are suitable: lean muscle

Foods to gnaw, including dog biscuits or air-dried strips of tripe, are crucial for keeping your dachshund's teeth and gums healthy.

meat, including beef, veal, venison, and horse meat. Poultry and fish (without the bones) are also good choices. For variety, you can also occasionally offer your dog; tripe, heart, liver, and kidneys.

Fat: Normally it is contained in sufficient quantities in meat. Only extra-lean meat has to be enriched with cold-pressed vegetable oil.

Grain products: Primarily whole-grain products are recommended. These are suitable when cooked: rice, corn, cereals, or noodles. Stale whole-grain bread or kibbled dog food are used uncooked.

Potatoes: They are always cooked (without salt) before serving.

Dairy products: Low-fat cottage cheese or farmer cheese can be used just as sold in the grocery store.

Vitamins and minerals: Minerals, trace elements, and vitamins are contained in the following home-prepared blend: ⅓ flaked brewer's yeast, ⅔ bone meal. Cut up raw fruit, vegetables, lettuce, or parsley, and add to the mix.

How Much Your Dachshund Should Eat

The daily amount of food depends not only on your dachshund's weight, but also on its individual requirements. The amount of exercise the dog gets plays a role here, as does its ability to utilize what it eats. The following suggested amounts, therefore, are meant only as guidelines. They are applicable to a healthy, full-grown dachshund:

Daily

- 60 percent protein, about 10.5 to 12.4 ounces (300–350 g) (meat, fish, farmer cheese, dairy products);
- 30 percent carbohydrates, about 5.3 to 7 ounces (150–200 g) (flaked dog food, grain, rice, potatoes, noodles);

- 5 to 10 percent fats, about 2 teaspoons (may already be contained in fattier meats);
- vitamins and minerals: 1 teaspoon.

Important: If you use kibbled dog food with added vitamins for your dog's meal, no additional dose of vitamins and minerals is necessary.

Preparation

Let the cooked ingredients cool thoroughly, then mix them with the other components of the dog's meal. Many dogs have a habit of "fishing out" the pieces of meat from their meal. In the long run, of course, that will result in nutritional deficiency symptoms that impair your pet's health. If your pet has that habit, try this little trick: Puree the dinner briefly in a blender. Be aware, however, that there is a chance that your dog will then reject the entire thing!

Additional Foods for Gnawing

Once or twice a week, give your dachshund something to gnaw on in addition to its home-prepared meals. That might include bones (see page 34), hard dog biscuits, or rawhide.

Training a Dachshund

Praise, not punishment and discipline, is the prime foundation of successful dog training. A dog should cooperate in its training, not obey commands out of fear.

Who Trains Whom?

In silent amusement, I have often wondered to what extent I have been trained by my dachshunds. Observe sometime how living with a dachshund is very gradually changing you. How, if you have been interpreting the notion of "neatness" somewhat loosely, you are now being trained by the young dog to be extremely neat, because it chews on any shoes left lying around or on whatever else it can find. Or how punctual you have suddenly become, because the little dog has to be taken outside at very well-defined intervals. Our "well-trained, obedient" dachshund has trained us subtly, just as thoroughly as we have trained it! Nonetheless:

Training Is Necessary

Only a well-trained dog is truly a pleasure to be with, and only an obedient dog can really be depended on. A lack of training also involves dangers for the dog, particularly in street traffic, but also in woods and fields, where a roaming or hunting dog might be shot accidentally by a hunter. From the very outset, great emphasis needs to be placed on training—particularly with the dachshund, of course, which has a reputation for being self-willed. That takes a great deal of time, patience, and firmness.

Basic Rules of Dog Training

1. Start the training as soon as the dog comes to your home to live.
2. First, you need to housebreak the dog (see page 22). Any other training objectives do not make sense until the dog is at least three months old.
3. Training won't work without some authority. If you don't set clear limits for the dog, and don't insist on having your way, there's a risk that the animal will not acknowledge you as pack leader and will refuse to obey.
4. Always use the same words (for example, "Let go," "No," "Phooey," "Bed," or "Come") for the same proceedings. That's the only way the young dog can grasp what the human sounds mean.
5. Praise and reprimands must always follow immediately on the heels of the dog's action; otherwise, it cannot see any connection between the events.
6. Use a friendly, gentle voice for praise, a stern voice for scolding. A dog has to learn very early that a short, firm "No!" is a prohibition to be respected.
7. If you should have to punish the dog, don't ever yell at it or hit it! The appropriate way to punish a dog is to pick it up by the scruff and shake it briefly. That is the same method female dogs use with their puppies.
8. Dachshunds need a great deal of activity and exercise. They like to be challenged, or they don't feel fully occupied. Make sure you don't ask too much of your pet!
9. Teach your puppy as much as possible while playing with it. Pleasant experiences will increase its readiness to obey.

For many, many years dachshunds have been used as hunting dogs.

HOW-TO: Training

Training a dog requires patience and firmness. The following exercises will show you how to teach the dog what it must know to survive and to share a house with you.

A Dog and Its Leash
Drawing 1

A dachsund must learn right away how to walk on a leash.

1. Walking your dog on a leash is one of the most important training exercises.

Getting Used to the Leash

At the outset, the little dog will be reluctant to have its freedom of movement restricted by the leash. As time passes, it is important to give it the feeling that the leash is its link to its master, not an instrument of torture. It is best to conduct the first few leash training sessions with the dog at home in familiar surroundings, in a playful way. First put the collar on, then the leash. Let the dog lead you, and don't pull on the leash. If the leash does tighten and your dachshund starts to resist, loosen up on the leash and talk soothingly to the dog. Encourage it to follow you. That usually is quite successful, because very young dogs that have just been separated from their mother need human contact. As soon as the dachshund comes to you, praise it and stroke it. It will gain two important experiences: It's good to come to my mistress (or master)! The leash is the link that makes this contact stronger! If the dog still resists violently, despite all your cajoling, you have to pull it closer to you very carefully, all the while saying soothing things like "That's a good dog." When it finally comes, reward it with a little treat. In this way all young dogs soon will get used to their collar and leash.

Walking on the Leash

Teach the dog not to tug on the leash by pulling it forcefully back to your side whenever it fights the collar too much. Then loosen the tension on the leash again. Every time the dog starts to tug, yank it back once more.

How to practice walking on a leash: Take the leash in your right hand, letting the dog walk at your left. If the dachshund moves along at your pace without pulling, that's a very good start.

Now change direction without giving a command, turning right, then back again. As you move the leash in front of you from right to left, the movement of your body can carry the dog along with it. If the dog follows your change of direction, the goal of the exercise is met.

"Sit"
Drawing 2

When it hears the command "Sit," the dog should sit down and not get up again until told to do so. This is important, for example, when you are crossing a street or when the dog has to wait for you outside a shop. You can practice this command during your daily walk. Keeping

2. The command "Sit" is practiced this way: Stop, pull lightly on the leash, and gently press your dachshund's rear end to the ground.

both hands on the leash, lessen your pace gradually and finally come to a stop. If your dog doesn't sit of its own accord, put a slight tension on the leash and, with your hand, gently push the dog's rear end down until your pet is seated. Then slacken the tension somewhat, while saying "Good dog—Sit." If the dog stays seated, praise it. If not, you need to repeat the exercise from the beginning. Upon hearing the command "Go," the dog can start walking again.

"Phooey"
Drawing 3

The command "Phooey" is to be used whenever you want the dog to stop what it is doing—for example, barking at every opportunity, jumping up on strangers, relieving itself indoors in the wrong place, stealing things, and so forth. The "Phooey" must be spoken emphatically, possibly even reinforced by clapping your hands as you speak. Remain firm! Even though your pet learns to yield to a stronger will, it will not lose its personality.

Staying in Its Bed
Drawing 4

"Bed" means that the dog should go to its own designated place to rest. For that to happen, the bed should be an object in which the dog feels comfortable. Moreover, your pet must have learned that the spot is its very own. How to demonstrate that to your dachshund: Once the lit-

3. "Phooey" means that the dachshund should refrain from doing something.

tle dog gives the first indication of being tired, take it to its basket. If necessary, keep it there a while by talking to it cajolingly, repeatedly saying and emphasizing the word "Bed." If it settles down, you can go away. If it gets up and leaves the basket, take it back at once, and keep repeating the word "Bed." Do this pleasantly and kindly, but be firm in insisting that it take its

nap in its own basket. If the dog feels safe and secure in its place, getting it used to staying there won't take long.

"Stay"
Staying Where It Is

Your dog should stay lying down even if you walk away from it. To teach your pet that lesson, hold your palm out in front of its face. If the dog stays where it is, praise it. This command is useful, for example, in the veterinarian's office when the dog needs to sit down on the examination table.

Staying in the Room

The command "Stay" is also used when you want the dog to stay in a room. Practice this as described above, by holding your palm out in front of your dog's face. Then pull your hand away and leave the room. Here it is important that the command "Stay" always be linked with the customary signal, the outstretched hand.

4. The command "Bed" tells the dog not to leave its place, even if you go away.

First, gently lick the angora rabbit's ear,

Following to Heel (Without Leash)

When the dog has learned to come when called and has mastered the command "Sit," and when walking on a leash has become second nature for it, you can begin practicing "walking without a leash." "Heel" is the command to use if you want the dog to follow closely behind you at the pace you dictate. So that the dog has as few distractions as possible, don't start practicing this in a busy street or near woods.

Coming When Called

A dog that is running around loose outdoors should come willingly when you call or whistle. That doesn't always happen right away, particularly when the dachshund reaches the age of six to seven months—"awkward adolescence." I always rewarded my dachshunds with a little treat and showered them with praise every time I called them to come. Once they noticed that coming to me was associated with something good, they immediately dashed up cheerfully. They continued to do so as the treats became increasingly smaller and finally ceased altogether, leaving only the affectionate words of praise. But until you reach that point, a young dachshund certainly can bring you to the point of rage by refusing to obey a single call or whistle. When it finally comes, it takes great self-control to be able to give the little creature some praise. If you give free rein to your anger at this point and scold the disobedient pup or perhaps even strike it with the leash, it will assuredly be even more disobedient the next time. The dachshund will interpret the experience in this way: "When I came back, I got scolded. So I'll take

then bite it tenderly,   *and now snuggle up to it.*

even more time or, even better, not go back at all, because I see how furious my top dog is."

The Command "Let Go"

Every dog has to learn that it must let go of whatever it has in its mouth—whether that be its food, a toy, or something it has found—at any time, and without resisting. That is absolutely essential when, during a walk in the country or in town, the dog picks up something that is not meant for it or, even worse, is dangerous for it. Letting go of something voluntarily is not exactly part of a dachshund's nature, but you need to teach your pet this command as early as possible. Otherwise, later on it will never let something be taken away from it again without resisting, perhaps even biting.

Use the command "Let go" when you want the young dog to let go of something and/or give you something immediately. Practice this with your puppy by taking away its toy. If it doesn't want to give it up right away, grab the dog from above, right above its little muzzle, and gently force its jaws apart. While doing so, say "Let go" loudly and insistently. As soon as you have the toy in your hand, give it back, and praise your pet. Almost all young dachshunds soon come to enjoy this game and give you whatever they have in their mouth as soon as they hear the command "Let go." You also can practice by taking your pet's food dish out from under its nose. If it growls at you, reprimand it with a forceful "Phooey." If it snaps at you, give it a perceptible swat (the most effective spot is the side of the muzzle). If that makes the dog

In the photos:
Dogs and rabbits are natural enemies, because the rabbit is one of the dog's traditional quarries. But friendships between animals sometimes take an unconventional path, as these photos prove. Nevertheless, it is not advisable to keep a rabbit together with a dog.

41

even angrier, grab it firmly by the scruff and scold it in a loud voice. You have to make it clear to the dachshund who is the leader of the pack. Once it gives in, praise it immediately with kind words and give its food back.

Practice this every day with your dog until the lesson sinks in and the dachshund obeys the command "Let go" even from a distance.

Do Dachshunds Make Good Family Dogs?

Are dachshunds really fond of children? That question can't be answered with a simple yes or no. No breed of dog fundamentally "loves children," nor does any breed inherently detest them. But there are certain breeds of dogs that I would not necessarily recommend to families with small or very young children. I do not believe that the dachshund is in that category, because aggression, nervousness, and sensitivity to noise in particular are generally not part of its makeup.

Whether a dog turns out to be friendly or hostile to children depends only to a minor extent on its individual disposition. Much more decisive are the experiences it has with children. If a dog of any breed is teased and tormented by children, it can scarcely harbor friendly feelings toward them. On the contrary, it will see every child as a menace, avoid being touched by children, and growl at or even bite any who try to touch it. How can we blame it for that? It's not the dog's fault that things turned out that way.

A Playmate or a Loner?

Among dachshunds, there are some less gregarious types that stay to themselves and reserve their affection solely for their own mistress or master. They don't harm anyone, but they want to be left in peace. Such dogs are less suitable for families with children. This kind of temperament is recognizable even in a puppy. Choose a cheerful, outgoing puppy that is friendly to you and your children. You are unlikely to have problems with such a dog (see How to Choose Your Puppy, page 17).

A Dog Is Not a Toy

Make it clear to your children over and over that a dog is not a toy, but an extremely lovable companion that occasionally needs to be left alone and not dragged around all the time. Naturally, the children may sometimes get scratched while romping with their dachshund. Some dogs snap when playing; the little teeth—particularly the sharp milk teeth—can inflict painful nips. None of this, however, should damage the relationship between the child and the dog. Children usually are extremely devoted to their four-legged friend.

If a Baby Is Expected

What happens if a young couple with a dachshund is expecting a baby? That need not create a problem. Dogs, however, can become jealous if they—once the center of the family's attention—suddenly are virtually ignored. Don't let that happen! Continue to give the dog its customary share of attention. Then the dachshund will very quickly accept the baby as a real part of the family, and often a friendship develops between the dog and the child that will endure for the rest of the dog's life.

Understanding Dachshunds

The Dog's Temperament and Behavior

Twelve thousand years of domestication have produced a great variety of dog breeds, as far as their appearance and nature are concerned. Despite this long association with humans, however, the patterns of a dogs' behavior still have much in common with those of their original ancestors, the wolves.

The wolf is a predatory animal—hence the dog's good hunting abilities. Because its territorial behavior is well developed, is a good protector.

As a pack animal, the dog feels comfortable only in a community. Consequently, it is well suited for sharing a companionable existence with humans. Its person and/or its family now become its pack. Within this pack the dog takes its place in a social hierarchy and acts in accordance with its laws. Always striving to improve its standing in the order of rank, the dachshund will put itself at the top if you don't show it clearly who the "pack leader" is.

Just as the dog makes itself understood within its pack, it also explains itself to its human family. To do so it uses two types of languages: articulate language and body language.

How Dogs Communicate with Each Other

Certain modes of a dog's behavior are not readily comprehensible to human beings, but they are an essential part of the dog's nature. If you tried to prevent it from developing those behavioral patterns, its well-being might be grievously disturbed. Such behaviors include:

Marking

As a rule, male dogs engage in this, but occasionally females also mark their territory by lifting a leg and urinating on a tree, bush, post, or something of the kind. They seek out elevated places like those in order to preserve the odor for as long as possible. In this way they mask the scent of another dog (see drawing, page 23).

Sniffing and Smelling

While we humans use our eyes and ears to orient ourselves, dogs get their information from the scents that they

A bone to gnaw. *To make it easier for the milk teeth to erupt, young dogs greatly enjoy chewing on firm objects—a rawhide bone, for example.*

sniff out so exhaustively on all sides. They also acquire information about other dogs by sniffing at them thoroughly. This follows an innate pattern:

Nose Contact

When two dogs meet for the first time, they begin by approaching each other with their muzzles thrust out, until their noses are almost touching. Then they sniff each other at length. Depending on whether they smell good or bad to each other, the relationship that develops will be either friendly or distant.

Checking the Anus

After nose contact comes so-called anal contact—the smelling of the other dog's rear end. It is a completely natural activity for a dog, because the glands located under the tail provide the animal with important information about its fellow. Scientists call this zone the "anal face." Only a self-confident dog will display it uncovered, with raised tail, to another dog.

Tip: To help your pet develop a healthy relationship with its peers, from time to time give it an opportunity to become acquainted with another dog. Get your dachshund used to such encounters while it is still young. Among full-grown dogs, this natural law applies: "One doesn't bite young dogs!" Only in this way can your dog learn the rules of canine etiquette.

What Else Dogs Do

Perhaps you have already observed how your dog buries something or rolls around in the dirt. This behavior is to be interpreted as follows:

Burying and Scraping

Burying bones probably is traceable to primeval times, when dogs were forced to save up a supply of them. Scraping or scratching before a dog lies down probably also dates from the same era, when, dogs first had to prepare a proper, comfortable, place on which to lie down in the grass or inside the cave.

Rolling in the Dirt

Dogs love to roll around in smelly, dirty places. In that way they mask their own scent and make themselves interesting to their fellow dogs.

Articulate Language

Dogs howl less than wolves, but they bark more. That is a consequence of domestication: After all, dogs were trained to guard and protect.

Barking can sound contented, enraged, or melancholy. Depending on the situation, it can express pleasure (playing, greeting) or warning (alertness, aggression).

Growling should be interpreted as a warning. Usually the dog also bares its teeth or bristles its hairs.

Yelping is usually associated with pain, but it also can be an expression of fear and distress.

Howling: Dogs will howl if they feel lonely, or in response to certain noises, including music, sirens, and the like.

Whimpering and whining are traceable to puppy language. In this way a dog indicates that it has some need—for example, that it has to go outside.

Dachshunds, like all other dogs, have many different methods of communicating with their fellow dogs and "their" humans. For that reason, it is important that dog owners recognize and correctly interpret the meaning of their dog's body language and vocal utterances.

From this vantage point, the dachshund has everything in its field of vision.

HOW-TO:
Body Language

How Dogs Communicate with Humans

Communication is an essential ingredient of the relationship between human and dog. Humans speak to their dogs in words and gestures, while dogs usually employ a combination of body language and articulate language (vocal utterances) to convey their mood or tell what they need. By careful observation, you can easily learn what your dog wants to say to you.

1. This attitude is the dachshund's way of saying "Play with me!"

Invitation to Play
Drawing 1

As often as possible, accept your pet's invitation to play. As a sign of increased alertness, it will prick up its ears. At the same time, it places its front legs on the ground, raises its rear end

slightly, and dances back and forth on its hind legs. Its eyes reveal happy excitement.

Gesture of Submissiveness
Drawing 2

If it lies on its back in front of you and relaxes, this should be taken as a gesture of trust, meaning "Please scratch me!"

If, however, the dog throws itself on its back while fighting with another dog, it is admitting defeat, as the weaker combatant. It is signaling to the other animal: "I give up!"

Servility

If the dog creeps along the ground with its tail tucked, it is displaying total subjugation.

Tail Position and Movement

A tail held horizontally expresses great contentment. A tail clasped between the legs indicates aloofness or fear. A tail held stiffly erect behind the dog is a sign of readiness to attack.

Rapid, vigorous wagging signals friendship. Nevertheless, don't take it for granted that a strange dog will let you touch it simply because it is wagging its tail: It may be "answering" your friendly words by wagging its tail, but that doesn't automatically mean that you can safely pet it. Never touch a strange dog unless you have its owner's expressed permission in advance! I want to stress this point—be sure to impress it upon your children! A dog lying down will show how much it likes you by slow, brief wagging or by thumping its tail on the ground.

2. If the dachshund lies down on its back, it wants to be scratched.

The Play of the Ears

Your dog also can use its ears to express a multitude of things. **Laid-back ears** always indicate that something is wrong. In an older, experienced dog it can actually be a sign of something very like a "bad conscience." The dog has done something that it knows from experience is sure to mean trouble. A dog may also put back its ears out of pleasure, however, but then it will wag its tail at the same time. In connection with a wagging tail, laid-back ears also express pleasure. **Cocked ears** mean increased alertness.

Ears put forward or turned to the side are an indication of readiness to attack.

Readiness to Attack
Drawing 3

A dog that is about to attack bares its teeth and growls. Its ears are thrust forward or turned to the side, and its tail is outstretched behind, unmoving.

Baring Its Teeth

Drawing 4

Pulled-back lips that expose all the dog's teeth signal the extreme alert phase: This animal will bite unhesitatingly!

Jumping Up

Many people think that jumping up and licking someone's face is a form of bad behavior in their dog, but the animal intends it as a sign of great friendliness. This is the way the dog greets "its people" and approaches them submissively. Incidentally, puppies greet their mother in this way, begging her to feed them.

Pawing

If your dog trustingly lays its paw on your knee or your arm, then paws at the air, it is begging for attention or food. This behavior is interpreted as a gesture of greeting and appeasement. It is derived from the puppy's efforts to get milk by kneading its mother's side with its paws while sucking at her nipples.

The Dog's Sensory Capacities

As far as a dog's sensory capacities are concerned, particularly the senses of smell and hearing, they are substantially superior to those of human beings. Over the course of thousands of years, humans have learned to take advantage of these properties and to develop a great many breeds with special abilities. For example, we have bred the dachshund to hunt, the St. Bernard to seek for missing

3. *This posture is a signal: "Watch out, I'm ready to attack."*

persons, and the German shepherd to search for traces of drugs.

Sense of Smell

A dog's nose is its most important sensory organ. It uses it to perceive its environment and to acquire an enormous variety of information. It can smell certain odors millions of times more keenly than we can. This enables the dachshund, for example, to pick up the scent of the quarry when hunting. It can scent the trail even if it was laid days earlier. The scent of another dog decides whether liking or antipathy will result. Dogs can even tell what mood "their" people are in by their scent.

Hearing

The dog's hearing ability is also far superior to ours. While we hear between 10,000 and 20,000 oscillations per second, a dog can pick up to between 70,000 and 100,000 oscillations per second. That makes the dog an excellent guard.

Sight

A dog's ability to see shapes and colors is somewhat limited; on the other hand, it sees better than we do at dawn or dusk. It also is able to perceive movement even in the dark.

4. *Bared teeth indicate that the dog is about to bite.*

If Your Dachshund Gets Sick

Initial Symptoms and Procedures

A dog can't tell you what's bothering it or where it hurts. Keep a close eye on your pet, because its appearance and behavior will give you clear signs if something is the matter. If your dog refuses to eat or is unusually thirsty, if it seems reluctant and listless, if it no longer likes being touched, if its eyes are slightly dull, if its coat seems distinctly changed, then something is wrong with it. Watch it closely and take it to the veterinarian as quickly as possible. Don't worry about making what may be an unnecessary trip to the veterinarian's office; it is better to make one trip too many than too few.

Information for the Veterinarian

To help your veterinarian arrive at a diagnosis, provide him or her with as exact as possible a description of the symptoms that have developed. Answers to the following questions are useful:

- When and what did the dog last eat?
- What about the feces?
- Has the dog vomited? Is it gagging?
- Does it have fever (see Taking Your Dog's Temperature, on this page)?
- Does it engage in any other unusual behavior, such as frequently shaking its head and scratching its ears or licking certain body parts?
- Does it have any injuries?
- Do certain movements cause it pain?

Taking Your Dog's Temperature

- Use a nonbreakable thermometer with a digital display. Smear some oil or lotion on the tip to lubricate it.
- The dog should be standing, and a second person needs to hold it still while you talk soothingly to it.
- Lift the dog's tail and insert the thermometer .8 inch (2 cm) into the dog's rectum.
- Remove the thermometer after one minute. If it reads over 102.2°F (39°C), the dog has a fever.

Administering Medicine

Dogs take many medications willingly, so you first need to see whether your dachshund will swallow its medicine voluntarily. If it refuses, you need to use force.

Tablets and pills can be concealed in some liverwurst or similar food and offered to your dog. It will swallow the morsel quickly, without noticing what it contains. If that doesn't work, you will have to force your pet's mouth open. If it clenches its teeth, gently press its chops against its teeth. First put the tablet as far back on the tongue as possible, then hold the dog's mouth closed. Check to see whether your pet really has swallowed its medicine.

With liquid medicine, carefully pull the lower lip out to form a pocket and pour the liquid—measured in advance—into it. Lift the dog's head slightly; that will force it to swallow. Disposable syringes (without a needle, of course) have proved quite helpful with this procedure (see drawing; page 51).

Most diseases are preceded by symptoms that your veterinarian can diagnose quickly and surely. Don't put off the trip to the veterinarian's office; the sooner the disease is identified, the less chance it has to spread.

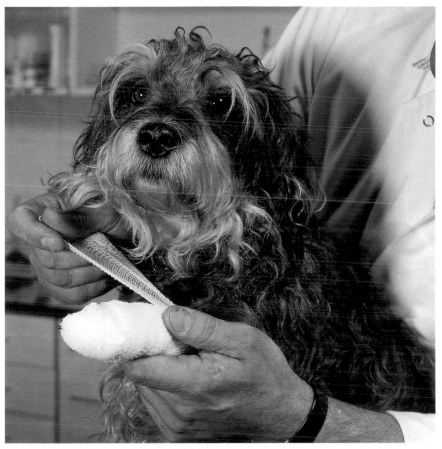

If your dachshund is ill, only a veterinarian can give it the expert treatment it needs.

Canine Diseases—Dangerous to Humans?

Just how dangerous are dog diseases to humans, and to what extent are they contagious?

Infectious diseases like rabies and a form of leptospirosis are communicable to humans. Vaccinated dogs pose no danger.

Parasites can also be transferred from dogs to humans. Small children, for example, can become infected with the eggs of roundworms through close contact with a dog that has not been wormed. Tapeworm eggs can also be transmitted to humans by a dog, playing the role of intermediate host. Fleas and ticks, which attack all warm-blooded creatures, can also be transferred from dogs to humans.

Fungal diseases are increasingly common. They can affect both humans and dogs, and they are mutually communicable.

Important Preventive Measures

Never fail to have your dog wormed and vaccinated. These procedures are extremely important in keeping your pet healthy, and they will help protect you as well!

Worm Treatments

You must have your dog freed from worms in order to keep it healthy.

Have it wormed at these ages:

- four weeks;
- six weeks;
- eight weeks (followed by first vaccination);
- 12 weeks (followed by second vaccination);
- six months;
- nine months;

After that, up the worming appointment so that it precedes each vaccination (see Vaccination Schedule), because the dog needs to be healthy when it gets its immunization injections.

Vaccination Schedule

To protect your pet against fatal diseases, you have to get it vaccinated. Each inoculation is entered in the dog's vaccination record, which you receive when you buy the dog.

Important: The dog should be wormed before every inoculation (see Worm Treatments).

Puppies should be vaccinated at the age of:

- eight to nine weeks, for distemper, hepatitis, leptospirosis, parvovirosis, and rabies.

Fully grown dogs should be vaccinated as follows, in alternate years:

- First year: Three-fold combination vaccine for leptospirosis, parvovirosis, and rabies (immunity to distemper and hepatitis lasts for at least two years).
- Second year: Five-fold combination vaccine for distemper, hepatitis, leptospirosis, parvovirosis, and rabies.
- Third year: Three-fold combination vaccine.
- Fourth year: Five-fold combination vaccine, and so forth.

Important: It is extremely important that the inoculations be repeated at regular intervals, so that immunity is maintained.

The Most Common Diseases

In the following material I have described diseases that occur with some frequency. Infectious diseases like distemper, rabies, hepatitis, leptospirosis, and parvovirosis now can be prevented by immunization (see Vaccination Schedule).

Vomiting

Cause: Vomiting can be quite harmless in dogs. If your dachshund has gulped its food too quickly or if there is something difficult to digest in its stomach, it may occasionally throw up. Vomiting once or twice is no cause for alarm, but if it is recurrent or is accompanied by fever, there may be a serious health problem. Vomiting and diarrhea may be a first indication of poisoning or infectious disease.

Treatment: If your dog vomits repeatedly, take it to the veterinarian.

Diarrhea

Cause: Often diarrhea results from an improper diet. Your dachshund may have been given too much liver. Milk—which full-grown dogs don't need but sometimes get—often has a strong laxative effect. Alternatively, your dog may simply have drunk overly cold water.

Treatment: If your pet suffers from diarrhea, give it some diluted black tea with a pinch of salt (drinking is important, to compensate for the loss of water) and put it on a special diet: oatmeal, rice porridge, and dry toast or zwieback, for example. If the diarrhea persists the next day, however, I recommend that you take your pet to the veterinarian.

Paralysis
Symptoms:
- stiff posture;
- obvious pain in the area of the cervical and lumbar vertebrae;
- unusual reluctance to move.

Cause: Because of the unnatural leverage involved—a long body on short legs—dachshunds' spines are subjected to a great deal of stress. In certain circumstances, this can result in prolapse of an intervertebral disk—a slipped or ruptured disk. Quick recovery may be possible, depending on the place in the spine where this occurs and on the seriousness of the problem. However, it can also result in paralysis of the dog's hindquarters. Older dogs usually are the ones affected.

Treatment: Because the symptoms are not always clearly recognizable and the trouble may suddenly go away again, you should take your dog to the veterinarian for an exact diagnosis at the first hint of disk problems. A cure—whether brought about by medication or by surgery—is possible only if the illness is spotted in time.

Distemper
Symptoms: Fever, vomiting, diarrhea, tonsillitis, coughing, watery eyes, in the advanced stage also muscle spasms and impaired mobility.
Cause: Virus.
Treatment: Usually fatal in young dogs. In full-grown dogs, the nervous system usually suffers permanent damage.

Administering medicine. *Medicine in liquid form is best administered with a disposable syringe (minus the needle).*

Prevention: Immunization (see page 50).

Leptospirosis
Symptoms: Usually begins with weakness in the hind legs. Other symptoms include fever, loss of appetite, vomiting, gastrointestinal problems, and tonsillitis. In serious cases, jaundice, impaired mobility, and foul mouth odor result.
Cause: Bacteria.
Treatment: Treatable in the early stage with antibiotics and immune serum.
Prevention: Immunization (see page 50).

Hepatitis
Symptoms: Fever, inflamed nasal and throat passages, vomiting, diarrhea, and a painful inflammation of the liver.
Cause: Hepatitis virus.
Treatment: Serum, antibiotics, and simultaneous artificial feeding may be successful. Puppies usually do not survive the disease, even with treatment.

Prevention: Immunization (see page 50).

Rabies

Symptoms: At first, abnormal behavior (moody, surly, often also affectionate, sensitive to light); later, frenzied biting, madness, difficulty swallowing accompanied by increased saliva flow. Final stage: total paralysis.
Cause: Viruses excreted along with the saliva of infected animals.
Treatment: Animals that have contracted rabies are untreatable.
Prevention: Immunization (see page 50).
Tip: Dogs that may have rabies are kept in quarantine under medical supervision. Because this disease also poses a threat to humans, anyone who may have come in contact with an animal suspected of having rabies has to undergo a series of inoculations immediately. Immunization of your dog is particularly important, because it is the only way to break the chain of communication from diseased wild animals to humans. In quarantined areas where rabies is present, I strongly urge that you have your pet immunized: Dogs running loose can be killed because they may have rabies. If you plan to travel abroad, your dog has to be vaccinated against rabies, and that information must be entered in its vaccination record.

Parvovirosis

Symptoms: Suddenly occurring foul-smelling bloody diarrhea, soon followed by severe vomiting, which also can become bloody with increased intensity. The dog becomes apathetic, refuses to eat, and runs the risk of severe dehydration ("drying out") because of the great loss of fluid.

Cause: Virus.
Treatment: Infusions and antibiotics. In puppies the disease is usually fatal.
Prevention: Immunization (see page 50).

Having Your Pet Put to Sleep

If your dachshund is incurably ill, seriously injured, or extremely frail and in constant pain that cannot be alleviated even with medical help, you should weigh the decision to have it put to sleep. Naturally it is not an easy decision to part from a faithful companion of many years, but remember that you will be sparing your pet further suffering and a painful death.

Being put to sleep is painless for the dog. It is injected with a large overdose of an anesthetic and goes to sleep peacefully. Stay with your little friend in its last minutes! Hold it in your arms or on your lap as it gets the injection that releases it from suffering. After so many years of friendship, you owe your dog this easy, painless death.

To keep the dog from pulling at its bandage and tearing it off, the veterinarian usually has it wear a high collar.

This sturdy, easy-to-clean carrier is handy if you have to take a sick dog to the veterinarian or if you want to take your pet along on a plane trip.

Health Problems

What You Notice	Possible Causes That You Can Remedy Yourself
Doesn't drink	Not enough moisture in food
Drinks a lot	Overheated after romping; has eaten a great deal of dry dog food
Diarrhea	Too much milk; cold food; has eaten snow; sudden change in diet; stress
Vomiting	Has eaten grass; has eaten too greedily; heartburn
Coughing	Choking, particularly along with drinking large amounts of water
Bad breath	Has eaten feces, carrion, or other foul-smelling matter
Flatulence	Diet of predominantly meat; sudden change in diet; doesn't tolerate type of dog food used
Straining without defecating or urinating	Constipation due to lack of exercise; too much dry dog food without drinking enough water; too many bones; labor pains
Labored breathing	Panting when overheated, exhausted, or excited

If Accompanied by These Symptoms, There Is Cause for Alarm	Possible Diagnosis and Treatment by Veterinarian
Drooling; swallowing the wrong way; coughing; gagging	Foreign object (bone) in throat; paralysis of throat (rabies); tonsil enlargement: See the vet at once!
Vomiting and subnormal temperature	Kidney damage (with uremia)
Apathy; staggering; subnormal temperature	Diabetes
In female, vomiting; fever; apathy; possibly vaginal discharge	Infection of uterus
Blood in feces; vomiting	Worm infestation; gastrointestinal infection; liver or pancreatic infection; poisoning: See the vet at once!
White and yellowish or bloody mucus	Gastritis; foreign object in stomach; liver or kidney disease; poisoning: See the vet at once!
Apathy; diarrhea; high fever	Serious viral infection (distemper; parvovirosis): See the vet at once!
Doesn't eat; no feces; taut abdomen	Foreign object in intestine: See the vet at once!
Dry cough with choking on mucus	Inflammation of tonsils, throat, or larynx (kennel cough)
Dry cough with gagging and in some cases bloody mucus	Foreign object or tumor in throat: See the vet at once!
Suppurating inflammation of conjunctiva and nose; labored breathing; fever	Cold; bronchitis; pneumonia (possibly distemper): See the vet at once
Wet, deep cough; labored breathing	Cardiac defect with lung blockage (cardiac asthma); pulmonary edema: See the vet at once!
Drooling, possibly with blood	Plaque; periodontal disease; festering tooth; foreign object (bone) or tumor in mouth
Vomiting; excessive thirst; foul breath that smells of urine	Gastritis; severe kidney disease with uremia
Diarrhea; light, pasty feces	Chronic pancreatic or liver disease
Particularly in a large dog: Gagging on mucus; abdomen inflated like balloon; total apathy; groaning breathing	Torsion of the stomach: See the vet at once; dog needs surgery within four hours!
Bloody mucus or blood from the anus	Constipation due to bone in feces (bone splinters in rectum): See the vet at once!
Bloody urine or dribbling urine	Stones in urethra or bladder: See the vet at once!
Fever; coughing; sneezing	Respiratory infection (kennel cough); pneumonia
Deep, wet cough; tachycardia	Cardiac defect with lung blockage (cardiac asthma); pulmonary edema: See the vet at once!
Pumping breath with ventral presses	Perforated lung or diaphragm: See the vet at once!
Pale mucous membranes, tachycardia	Internal bleeding after accident or poisoning: See the vet at once!

If Your Dog Has Puppies— Dachshund Breeding

Normally a female dachshund takes care of her puppies herself for the first four weeks. From the fifth week of life on, you need to provide the little pups with additional food, and it is also time to have them wormed.

Heat

Female dogs, or bitches, come into heat every six to ten months. Estrus, as this period is also known, lasts about three weeks. In a young female dog, it first occurs at the age of seven to nine months. Restlessness and increased appetite are signs of its approach. This period naturally presents a few problems for dog owners. In particular, you need to protect your bitch from undesirable male dogs that are attracted by her odor and sometimes literally besiege her.

To prevent your dog from leaving spots of blood throughout your house during estrus, put a pair of special pull-up diapers (available in pet stores) on her.

Tip: You can suppress estrus with a hormone injection or an operation, but don't do so until after the dog is full-grown.

Pregnancy and Whelping

The gestation period lasts about 60 to 65 days. During this time the female needs to eat two to three times her normal amount. Make sure that her food contains plenty of minerals, trace elements, and vitamins. Suitable commercial blends are available in pet stores. While the dog is nursing, "puerperal tetany," or eclampsia, can occur. In these conditions, as a result of a breakdown in the body's metabolism of calcium, severe convulsions occur, followed by difficulty in breathing that can lead to heart failure if treatment is delayed. Dogs that are especially good milk producers are at greatest risk. Make sure your female has enough calcium in her diet both before she gives birth and while she is nursing.

Late in her pregnancy, when the bitch starts building a nest, you should prepare a whelping box for her. These boxes are sold in pet stores, but, if necessary, a wooden crate with low sides will also do. Line the bottom with several layers of newspaper, cover them with a blanket, and on top of that put several soft, absorbent cloths that can be changed as necessary.

Particularly with the small breeds, complications in giving birth are not uncommon. Small dogs usually do not have large litters (as far as the number of puppies is concerned). The fewer puppies there are, however, the larger the individual offspring are, and that can make for a difficult birth. Be sure never to leave your dog alone when she is whelping. The intervals between the individual births should never exceed one hour. If you sense that there are problems, call the veterinarian.

Don't Forget: Training Starts with the Newborn Pup

Watch carefully someday how animal mothers prepare their young for life. Through playing with them they teach them proper behavior—but they also insist that the growing pups obey and they punish them in no uncertain terms if they refuse. Training is indispensable. Anyone who lives in a community has to learn to fit in. That also applies to

During the first few months of life, the puppies don't leave their mother's side.

dogs, which are pack animals. When we then bring our puppy home at an age of a few weeks, we are—understandably—completely won over by the charming little creature that snuggles in our arms for protection. "We can't start training such a little animal so soon," you may think. But it is precisely young dogs that are especially receptive; they learn easily and quickly. For this reason, start the training process early—within reasonable lim-

its, of course. It is particularly important that you be quite clear about who is going to be the puppy's principal trainer. Nevertheless, the other members of your family also have to learn to use the same words with the dog, so that it hears identical orders from everyone. Training and teaching a young dog properly is a great deal of fun—but it takes time, time, and more time (see Training Dachshunds, page 36).

Breeding

If you, as the owner of a female dachshund, wish to raise puppies, you need to ask yourself whether you also meet the prerequisites for doing so. A breeder needs not only a great deal of experience in keeping dogs, but also a lot of time. In addition, suitable premises and an appropriate exercise area have to be available.

Not all dachshunds are suitable for breeding. That issue needs to be settled in advance by a judge who reviews the dog from the standpoint of breeding. If your dog rates a "Very good" or "Outstanding," you can proceed with your plans.

With unsupervised reproduction there is a risk that the offspring will be degenerate dogs with poor character and weak nerves or mongrels that no one wants to buy.

Breeding is a subject that you should investigate thoroughly. If you seriously intend to breed dachshunds, you should join the American Dachshund Club (see Useful Addresses, page 63). The club will advise you on everything pertaining to breeding, and may even help you find a suitable male animal for your female.

Rules for Breeding and Testing

The prerequisite for all planned animal husbandry is a clear breeding objective. Every breeder has the right to freely choose a partner for his or her dog within the limits of the existing regulations.

In general, Europeans have stricter rules than Americans. We have elected the German Dachshund Club as the European representative, and will at times compare their ways with those of the American Dachshund Club and the American Kennel Club.

As we saw on page 6, the American Dachshund Club recognizes three coat types and two sizes, whereas the Germans recognize the three coats but have three sizes. They do not allow crosses between the different coat types and different sizes, while the Americans merely indicate that certain crosses are to be discouraged, e.g., crossing a long-haired with a wirehaired.

Prerequisites for breeding: The chief U.S. prerequisites for breeding are the sound health, good development, and impeccable character of the breeding animal. Because dachshunds have been used for hunting since our great-grandfathers' day, their powerful bodies should be muscular and their facial expressions challenging. Fearful dogs with character weaknesses should not be used for planned breeding. These characteristics, however, are apparent only in full-grown animals. For that reason, a dachshund should not be bred until it is completely grown; that is, until it is 15 months old.

Dachshunds that are to be bred also should be free from congenital defects and hence fit for use as breeding stock. All of the above prerequisites must be followed in most European countries; otherwise the owner will not be able to receive a legal permit to breed.

Studbook regulations: In addition to these basic prerequisites, there are detailed regulations that govern the entry of dogs in the studbook of the American Kennel Club or the German Dachshund Club.

The studbook is open to any dachshund breeder, provided the dog and then her first litter are registered and the owner acknowledges and follows the regulations.

Any dachshund bred in this country is eligible for inclusion in the studbook. Its pedigree must be proved beyond a shadow of a doubt. In most European countries, the dog must also have been vaccinated for distemper, hepatitis, leptospirosis, and, if possible, parvovirosis (see Vaccinations, page 50). Dogs imported from abroad are entered in the studbook only if the pedigrees of the dogs are issued by the appropriate FCI studbook registry abroad. In Europe, offspring of dachshunds imported from abroad are entered in the studbook only if the pedigrees of both parents are issued by a studbook registry abroad that is affiliated with the Federation Cynologique Internationale (FCI). Excluded from entry in the studbook are dachshunds that:

- result from crossing of the different coat types (applies to Europe only);
- have no valid proof of pedigree (U.S. and Europe);
- come from breeders that have been barred from the studbook (Europe only);
- have been bought and sold by pet dealers (Europe only).

If you want more information, contact the American Kennel Club (see Useful Addresses, page 63).

Breeding Reviews and Exhibitions

The German and American Dachshund Clubs support efforts to breed dachshunds with perfectly shaped bodies and, especially in Europe, to preserve and cultivate the exhibitions.

It should be noted that in the United States the emphasis always has been on the conformation of the dog, whereas in Europe this interest is shared with a strong desire to test the abilities of the dachshund as a working dog. That is why tests to determine a dog's suitability for use in hunting are conducted throughout Europe. The examination subjects are:

- gun-shyness test;
- water test;
- baying (giving tongue, "singing") test;
- perspiration test;
- game starting (rousing, bolting, putting up) test;
- versatility test.

This extremely difficult examination is also called the "dachshund's final exam." There are two more special tests for dwarf and rabbit dachshunds:

- ability to pull out a rabbit drag (scent bag);
- natural ability to start (unearth) a rabbit;

Further details of these tests are, again, available from the German Dachshund Club (see Useful Addresses, page 63).

Playing. *Dachshund puppies practice patterns of canine behavior while playing with their siblings. The relative strength displayed during play can later determine the dog's rank within the pack.*

Index

Useful Addresses

American Kennel Club
51 Madison Avenue
New York, NY 10010
(212) 696-8200

Dachshund Club of America, Inc.
c/o Walter M. Jones
390 Eminence Pike
Shelbyville, KY 40065
(502) 633-9277

Dachkelclub Deutschland
(German Dachshund Club)
c/o Helmut Kamphaus
Donnerstrasse 139-141
W-4300 Essen 1 Germany

Veterinary Pet Insurance
1-800-USA-PETS
In California: 1-800-VPI-PETS

Useful Books

For further reading on this subject
and related matter, consult the following books also published by
Barron's Educational Series, Inc.,
250 Wireless Boulevard,
Hauppauge, NY 11788:

Fiedelmeier L.: *Dachshunds,* 1984.
Klever U.: *The Complete Book of
Dog Care,* 1989.
Alderton D.: *The Dog Care Manual,*
1986.
Frye FL.: *First Aid for Your Dog,*
1987.
Baer T.: *How to Teach Your Old
Dog New Tricks,* 1991.
Baer T.: *Communicating with Your
Dog,* 1989.
Eldridge W.: *The Best Pet Name
Book Ever,* 1990.
Ullman HJ.: *The New Dog
Handbook,* 1984.

The Photographers

IPO: page 33; Junior/Grell: front
cover; Junior/Liebold: inside front
cover/1, 8/9; Nicaise: pages 16, 29,
45, back cover; Schendel: page 32;
Wegler: pages 4, 20, 24, 37, 40, 41,
49, 53, 64, inside back cover;
ZEFA/Spichtinger: page 13;
ZEFA/Wegler: page 57.

Cover Photos

Front cover: Wirehaired dachshund.
Inside front cover: Four longhaired
dachshund puppies. Inside back
cover: Various coat types and colors.
Back cover: Smooth-coated, longhaired, and wirehaired dachshunds.

Sources

The chapter titled "Proper Nutrition"
was written by Christine Metzger.
The table "Health Problems" was the
work of Uwe Streitferdt.

© Copyright 1993 by Gräfe und Unzer
GmbH, Munich.
The title of the German book is *Dackel.*
Translated from the German by Kathleen
Luft.

First English language edition published in
1994 by Barron's Educational Series, Inc.
English translation © Copyright 1994 by
Barron's Educational Series, Inc.

Address all inquiries to:
Barron's Educational Series, Inc.
250 Wireless Boulevard
Hauppauge, NY 11788

Library of Congress Catalog Card
No. 94-1091

International Standard Book
No. 0-8120-1843-5

**Library of Congress Cataloging-in-
Publication Data**
Fiedelmeier, Leni.
[Dackel. English]
Dachshunds : how to take care of them
and understand them : expert advice on
proper care / Leni Fiedelmeier : with
color photos by well-known animal
photographers : drawings, Fritz W.
Kohler : consulting editor, Frederic Frye.
p. cm.
"A Barron's pet owner's manual."
Includes bibliographical references
and index.
ISBN 0-8120-1843-5
1. Dachshunds. I. Title.
SF429.D25F52713 1994
636.7'53—dc20
94-1091
CIP

PRINTED IN HONG KONG
567 9927 987654

Important Notes

This Barron's pet owner's manual tells the reader how to buy and
take care of a dachshund. The author and the publisher consider it
important to point out that the guidelines suggested in this book
apply primarily to normally developed puppies from a good breeder—that is, healthy dogs of good character.

Anyone who adopts a full-grown dog needs to be aware that the
animal has already been considerably influenced by human beings.
You should watch the dog very carefully, particularly its behavior
toward humans. If possible, meet the previous owner. If the dog
comes from an animal shelter, someone on the staff may be able to
give you information about the dog's background and peculiarities.
There are dogs that, as a result of bad experiences with humans,
behave in an odd manner or perhaps even tend to bite. Such dogs
should be adopted only by experienced dog owners. Even well-
trained and carefully supervised dogs on occasion damage someone
else's property or, even worse, cause accidents. It is in the owner's
interest to have adequate insurance protection; we strongly urge that
you purchase a liability insurance policy to cover your pet.

Coat Types, Sizes, and Colors

Today dachshunds are bred in three different coat types: shorthaired (smooth); longhaired; and wirehaired. The same is true of the sizes. In the United States, these can be standard (over 16 pounds) or miniature (11 pounds or less, at less than one year of age). In Europe, especially in Germany, there are three categories: standard dachshunds; dwarf dachshunds, whose chests can measure up to 14 inches (35 cm) around; and "rabbit dachshunds," whose chest circumference may reach up to 12 inches (30 cm). Because fur colors also vary, there are one-colored dachshunds, two-colored dachshunds, and spotted (dappled, sable) dachshunds.

Wirehaired dachshund, wild pig-colored (brindle).

Longhaired dachshund, red (tan) with appressed silky hair.

Smooth dachshund, black-and-tan.

The fur of a short-haired dachshund should be short, thick, shiny, and smooth. If bald areas appear anywhere on the body, the dog does not conform to the breed standard set forth by the Dachshund Club of America and the German Dachshund Club.

Longhaired dachshunds should have a silky, shiny coat of hair. Markedly curly, wavy, or, even worse, straggly hair is considered a fault according to the breed standard.

Dwarf longhair, black sable coat.